"Mark DeVine has provided a most important service for the Christian community at-large with this illuminating work on Dietrich Bonhoeffer. This volume provides an insightful and well written account of Bonhoeffer's life and work. Moreover, DeVine combines his historical interpretation with compelling applications for the church of our day. I heartily recommend this significant publication."

David S. Dockery
President, Union University

"Here is a fresh, accurate and compelling portrayal of Bonhoeffer, his life and thought, written by a bright Southern Baptist theologian who knows his subject well. Mark DeVine makes Bonhoeffer come alive and commends him as a tonic for today's self-satisfied church that needs to learn again the meaning of obedience, discipleship, community, suffering, and hope."

Timothy George
Dean, Beeson Divinity School at Samford University
Executive Editor, *Christianity Today*

D0813422

BONHOEFFER

Speaks TODAY

BONHOEFFER
Speaks TODAY

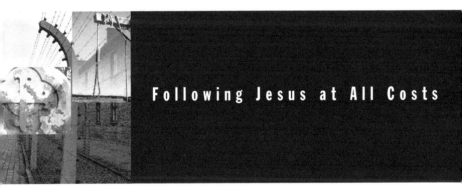

Following Jesus at All Costs

MARK DEVINE

BROADMAN
&HOLMAN
PUBLISHERS

NASHVILLE, TENNESSEE

Ten-Digit ISBN: 0–8054–3261–2
Thirteen-Digit ISBN: 978–0–8054–3261–9

Published by Broadman & Holman Publishers
Nashville, Tennessee

Dewey Decimal Classification: 261
Subject Heading: CHRISTIAN LIFE \
BONHOEFFER, DIETRICH \ CHRISTIAN SOCIOLOGY

Scripture quotations are from The Holy Bible, English Standard
Version, copyright © 2001 by Crossway Bibles, a division of Good
News Publishers. Used by permission. All rights reserved.

1 2 3 4 5 6 7 8 9 10   10 09 08 07 06 05

for
my wife, Jackie
sine qua non

CONTENTS

ACKNOWLEDGMENTS

I WISH TO THANK Mary Glazener, whose appreciation of Bonhoeffer inspired my own interest in his life and work. I also thank my wife, Jackie, and my assistant, Mindy Rose, for proofreading the manuscript and my colleague Dr. Michael McMullen, at whose suggestion I submitted the initial proposal. I also wish to thank the president and trustees of Midwestern Baptist Theological Seminary for granting an academic sabbatical during which much of the research for this project was completed. Thanks are due also to my editor John Landers and to Judi Hayes.

INTRODUCTION

I N   T H I S   V O L U M E I shall attempt to make Bonhoeffer speak to us today.
More specifically, I shall endeavor to exploit aspects of Bonhoeffer's
life and work that speak to concerns relevant to evangelical Christians.
Defining *evangelical* presents significant difficulties, but for our purposes British historian David Bebbington's four indicators will suffice:
evangelicals are marked by concern for conversion, the Bible, evangelism, and Christ. Evangelicals claim an experience with the living
Christ by which they have been converted to become his followers.
This experience is often called the new birth. Evangelicals are further
marked by acknowledgment of the Bible as the authoritative Word
of God. Evangelical doctrine and practice should arise from and be
judged by the writings of the Old and New Testaments. Evangelicals
accept the happy duty to proclaim the gospel of Jesus Christ through
which they hope for converts. Finally, evangelicals emphasize Jesus
Christ, his person and his work, as the central, perfect, and eternal
revelation of God to humanity. In any case, my purpose here is not

to engage the question of how to place Bonhoeffer within the history of theology, but to make Bonhoeffer help us evangelicals follow Jesus today. I think he can.

chapter one

AT ALL COSTS

"when Christ calls a man,
he bids him come and die."[1]

DIETRICH BONHOEFFER

FABIAN VON SCHLABRENDORFF began experimenting with explosives in February 1943. The assassination of Adolf Hitler would be attempted. Schlabrendorff quickly rejected the German-made bombs because of the hissing sound they made prior to detonation. Dietrich Bonhoeffer—pastor, nonviolent resister, children's Sunday school teacher, and pacifist—prayed for Schlabrendorff's success. How had it come to this? Was the author of *The Cost of Discipleship* able to pursue Jesus Christ and the death of a dictator at the same time? Did the first pursuit finally compel the other? What does it mean to be a child of heaven while living on this earth? Dietrich Bonhoeffer faced such questions without the luxury of time. World-altering events demanded decision from those living within the explosive cauldron of Hitler's Third Reich.

The Silver Spoon

Dietrich Bonhoeffer was born, along with his twin sister Sabine, on February 4, 1906, in Breslau (present-day Wroclaw, Poland) into an impressive aristocratic family. Among the Bonhoeffers, precociousness in children was usual, expected as a matter of course. Accomplished musicians, lawyers, physicians, ministers, and scientists punctuated both paternal and maternal family lines. His father Karl, professor of neurology and psychiatry at Berlin from 1912, was arguably among the five most prominent psychiatrists in the world. Having relocated to Berlin when Dietrich was six years of age, the Bonhoeffers' neighbors included many noted figures, among others the famous physicist Max Planck and the celebrated church historian and theologian Adolf von Harnack, who would later become Dietrich's teacher.

As to the expected precociousness, Dietrich did not disappoint. He was playing Mozart's sonatas at the age of ten and was expected by many to pursue a career in music. As a young student Bonhoeffer immersed himself in philosophy, history, Greek, and Hebrew with unusual zeal. Much of his early education was provided by tutors at home, and Dietrich was able to skip years of school by virtue of his intellect and industry. Sports and games became outlets for his intense competitiveness, which he also expected and celebrated in others. From childhood, conspicuous seriousness and intensity characterized Bonhoeffer's approach to life in every dimension.

Dietrich also marched to the beat of his own drummer. One classmate remembered the impression Bonhoeffer made during Harnack's last seminar at the University of Berlin: "I was struck by Dietrich Bonhoeffer, not only because he outdid practically all of us in theological knowledge and ability . . . but because here was someone who thought for himself and already knew what he wanted and also wanted what he knew."[2] Owing partly perhaps to his being the sixth of eight children with a separation of five years from his next oldest brother but, no doubt, chiefly because of his own particular constitution, Dietrich consistently asserted his independence. He was always standing for something.

Though his mother was a Christian believer and incorporated religion into the household routine, his father and brothers were largely agnostic, and the family rarely darkened the door of the church. Yet, at no later than age fourteen, young Dietrich announced that he would become a theologian. Considering the prominent ministers among his forebears, such a decision should not have come as the shock it did. His family, especially his male siblings, urged him to reconsider, begging their baby brother not to squander his life in such a "poor, feeble, boring, petty, bourgeois institution as the Church." "If what you say is true," Bonhoeffer retorted, "I shall reform it!"[3]

Bonhoeffer took immense pleasure in the benefits of his aristocratic upbringing but also felt keenly his separation from those he called "the others." Bonhoeffer's discomfort with a purely academic life and his periodic plunges into hands-on ministry reflect a deep desire to identify with humankind in ways he suspected his privileged station in life had denied him. Still, young Dietrich discovered soon enough that, for the Bonhoeffers, cultural and material privilege did not provide escape from duty and sacrifice. When Dietrich was only twelve years old, two of his brothers, Karl-Friedrich and Walter, enlisted as volunteers in the Great War. On April 23, 1918, Walter was wounded; and, five days later, following an operation, he died. Grief gripped the Bonhoeffer household, sending the bereaved mother, Paula, into a prolonged depression and leaving a profound mark on Dietrich.

Bonhoeffer the Student and Scholar

At age seventeen Bonhoeffer matriculated at Tübingen to study theology. There he concentrated especially on philosophy and textual criticism and earned a reputation as a brilliant, competitive, and independent soul possessed of sharp wit—poised to tease but also ready to make himself the object of his own pointed humor. He joined the Swabian fraternity Hedgehog, which later accepted the insertion of the Aryan Clause into its constitution, prompting Dietrich's withdrawal. During this time Dietrich apparently gave little attention to the fierce public debate raging in the pages of the widely circulated periodical journal *Christliche Welt* (The Christian World) between the Bonhoeffers' famous neighbor Adolph von Harnack and Swiss theologian at Göttingen, Karl Barth. Within a year, Bonhoeffer's encounter with the theology of Barth would permanently set him on a course opposed to the liberalism of Harnack and toward a more dogmatic, more conservative, biblical trajectory in his thinking.

Rome

After his first term at Tübingen, Bonhoeffer sustained a serious injury while ice skating. Following his recovery, he spent the next term in Rome where, for the first time, Roman Catholicism made a deep and lasting impression on him. The antiquity and universality

of the church impressed him as he explored Catholic Rome and Vatican City. A certain weightiness and sense of the permanence of the church extended in time and space, along with an exalted spiritual unity, seemed to inhabit the place. The Protestant church appeared narrow and provincial in comparison. The following excerpt from a sermon preached four years later to an expatriate German community in Barcelona captures something of the effect Rome had on the young Bonhoeffer:

> There is a word that when a Catholic hears it kindles all his feelings of love and bliss; that stirs all the depths of his religious sensibility, from dread and awe of the Last Judgment to the sweetness of God's presence; and that certainly awakens in him the feeling of home; the feeling that only a child has in relation to its mother, made up of gratitude, reverence and devoted love; the feeling that overcomes one when, after a long absence, one returns to one's home, the home of one's childhood.
>
> And there is a word that to Protestants has the sound of something infinitely commonplace, more or less indifferent and superfluous, that does not make their heart beat faster; something with which a sense of boredom is so often associated, or which at any rate does not lend wings to our religious feelings—and yet our fate is sealed if we are unable again to attach a new, or perhaps a very old meaning to it. Woe to us if that word does not become important to us soon again, does not become important in our lives.
>
> Yes, the word to which I am referring is "Church," the meaning of which we [Protestants] have forgotten and the nobility and greatness of which we propose to look at today.[4]

Nevertheless, Bonhoeffer's encounter with Catholicism did not strip him of his critical faculties. Amazingly, he gained an audience with the pope, who proved to be a keen disappointment. Moreover, Bonhoeffer engaged in spirited theological debate with a Catholic priest. Still, this brief stay in Rome stoked the fires of interest in things ecclesiastical, which would account for a good part of Bonhoeffer's enduring contribution to all believers longing for rich fellowship within the church.

Bonhoeffer and Barth

Bonhoeffer never willingly surrendered to strong personalities. The only mentors to whom he granted real authority over him were Professor Karl Barth, and Dr. Bell, the bishop of Chichester. His discovery of Barth took place between the summers of 1924 and 1925, after his trip to Rome but before he commenced work on his thesis. Prior to his move to Münster in October 1925, Barth had been lecturing at Göttingen where Bonhoeffer's cousin Hans-Christoph von Hase became so smitten with him that he transferred to the school of theology. A bitter debate between Barth and Harnack had been carried on in the periodical *Christliche Welt* in 1923. In the end Bonhoeffer would find himself increasingly alienated from the liberalism represented not only in his supervisory professor, Reinhold Seeberg, but also in his neighbor, Harnack.

Barth's 1919 theological commentary on Romans, the so-called bomb dropped into the playground of theologians, marked the beginning of a major attack upon Protestant liberalism and the attempt to recover Reformation theology for the modern world. While concern for the church captivated Bonhoeffer's attention, the Barthian revolution centered on the recovery of the revelation of God and the Bible.

Nevertheless, certain insights found in Barth emerge again and again in the Bonhoeffer corpus. One was dogmatism, that is, the rejection of felt relevance as the starting point of theology. Bonhoeffer's embrace of strong Reformation doctrine of sin led to suspicion of essentially apologetic approaches taken by, for example, Rudolf Bultmann and eventually by Paul Tillich. The God of the Bible not only prescribes medicine for sin-sick souls and congregations but diagnoses as well. Another was the centrality of the Bible for the church as its guide and authority both for preaching and for congregational life.

Ministry

Bonhoeffer advanced along the path toward a teaching career with exceptional speed, and yet, increasingly, he questioned whether his true calling centered upon academic life. From very early on, Bonhoeffer harbored deep interest in active ministry. At the tender age of twenty-one, while under the extraordinary demands of his doctoral thesis, Bonhoeffer sought to satisfy the qualifications prerequisite to parish ministry. This process included not only theological examinations but also proof of practical ministry experience. Accordingly Bonhoeffer accepted responsibility for the children's Sunday school at Grunewald. Bonhoeffer invested himself completely in the lives of these children, entertaining them frequently at his home, organizing many extracurricular outings and Bible studies for them. Surprisingly, he became alarmed when the children became so quickly attached to him and the influence he had on them. Not unlike the experience of Karl Barth during his pastorate at Safenwil fourteen years earlier, Bonhoeffer felt keenly the responsibility borne by one received as a minister of the Word of God.

Periodically, for the rest of his life, Bonhoeffer underwent similar experiences. Often, when some recognition or success came to him, he found himself confronted with his black heart, the sin of pride he knew to be present just beneath the surface of consciousness, and he contemplated with horror the thought that others looked up to him. How like Luther! And how incompatible with the optimistic anthropology so prevalent among his teachers, with the notable exception of Barth. This disgust with himself that assaulted him throughout his life had much in common with the temptations (*anfechtungen*) suffered by Martin Luther. No doubt, such tangible, experiential acquaintance with one's sinful heart and mind fueled Bonhoeffer's lifelong clinging to salvation by grace alone.

In order to fulfill the two-year parish ministry requirement, Bonhoeffer made his way to Barcelona, Spain, to serve the expatriate German community there. Though the congregation consisted mainly of business people, Bonhoeffer's ministry also brought him into contact with, in his words, "the strangest people, with whom one would not normally have exchanged a single word: bums, vagabonds, criminals fleeing from justice, many foreign legionaries, lion-tamers and animal-trainers who have absconded from the Krone circus on its Spanish tour . . . . We are constantly arranging passages home for Germans, even though we know the situation is no better there."[5] Bonhoeffer claims not to have had a theological conversation for an entire year.

Here lies a key to Bonhoeffer's emerging ministerial identity; these plunges into active ministry were not viewed as distractions but as the true testing ground for whatever one thought one knew from books. For Bonhoeffer, theory must prove itself in practice. And yet such serious respect for lived-out Christianity never suggested an empty-headed ministerial ideal. After returning to Berlin to join the theological faculty there, Bonhoeffer continued to reflect on his future: "I feel that academic work will not hold me for long. But I do think that as thorough an academic grounding as possible is all-important."[6]

In 1930 Bonhoeffer traveled to New York for a year as an exchange student. His experiences there left an indelible mark on him. Once again Bonhoeffer found himself pulled in two directions at once—toward academics and toward the worshipping congregation. Germans tended to patronize American seminaries because of their neglect of historical theology in favor of ethics. Classmates at Union Theological Seminary in Manhattan found Bonhoeffer's reference to a passage on sin and forgiveness from Luther's *Bondage of the Will* funny. Students seemed wholly ignorant of the theology running from the apostle Paul through Luther, Kierkegaard, and Barth. Still, Bonhoeffer was favorably impressed with the this-worldly focus and particularly of the distinct brand of Christian pacifism and nonviolence he encountered.

As to concrete engagement with the church, Bonhoeffer found himself enthralled with the African-American congregations in Harlem and moved by the special struggle for racial equality he witnessed. Bonhoeffer left New York more politically alert and more interested in ecumenical concerns. He returned to a Germany just beginning to grapple with the landslide victory of the National Socialist Party in elections held during his absence. German politics would hold Bonhoeffer's attention for the rest of his days.

Between 1931 and 1936 Bonhoeffer served as a university lecturer at the University of Berlin. But his teaching duties accounted for only a small portion of his labor. Bonhoeffer threw himself into ecumenical activity, preaching, and various conference work with amazing zeal and abandon. Bonhoeffer's ecumenical interest was more an expression of loyalty to Christ and his followers above allegiance to

Germany; it certainly did not arise from any latent doctrinal latitudinarianism or indifference.

Upon his return to Germany, Bonhoeffer finally initiated the first of many meetings with the most important theological teacher of his life, Karl Barth. After the first personal encounter in Bonn, Bonhoeffer wrote of his impressions to a Swiss friend

It is important and, in the nicest way, astonishing to see that there is even more to Barth than his books. He has a frankness, a willingness to listen to criticism, providing that it is relevant, and at the same time such concentration and a violent insistence on the subject whether it is discussed with arrogance or modesty, dogmatically or quite tentatively. . . . I am even more impressed by his conversation than by his writings and lectures. Here you really see the whole man.[7]

The content of Bonhoeffer's lectures during these years displayed an eclectic quality indicative of his youth, but also bore the stamp of his own distinctive combination of emphases that had percolated in his mind from his teenage years. Political engagement, ecumenism, and pacifism grew increasingly conspicuous over these years. Theologically, from Barth, one notices the prominence of the doctrine of revelation, the recovery of Bible, dogmatics versus apologetics, and the centrality of Jesus Christ. Against Barth, one detects a certain anti-Calvinist bent, leaning more toward Luther, especially regarding discipleship and the broader issues bearing on the Christian life. As to piety and churchmanship, Bonhoeffer surprised his students by opening his classes with prayer and encouraging them to adopt a daily regime of personal prayer and meditation on passages from Holy Scripture. During this period Bonhoeffer made his life-changing "discovery of the Bible," which we will explore more fully below.[8]

Political events increasingly impinged on Bonhoeffer's ability to study, debate, and engage in serious research as he would have liked. During the late 1920s the desire for an authoritarian order grew among the right-wing bourgeoisie within Germany. Hitler came to power on January 30, 1933. Within two years Bonhoeffer was already beginning to face the deadly seriousness of the situation: "We should not be surprised if the time comes for our church too, when the blood of martyrs will be called for."[9]

On the evening of February 27, while Chancellor Hitler enjoyed a dinner hosted by the soon to be named propaganda chief, Joseph Goebbels, news came that the *Reichstag* (German Parliament) was on fire. Hitler immediately blamed the Communists, insisting that an incipient revolution must be stamped out before it was too late. From late February through March, with this pretext of a developing emergency, fateful laws came streaming forth from the newly empowered Third Reich: the Treachery Law made opposition to the government tantamount to treason; the Enabling Act abrogated the power of the Parliament and the constitution; the Decree for the Reconstruction of Professional Civil Service, the so-called non-Aryan law, began the declassification of one group by race; the Edict for the Protection of the People and State, the so-called "Reichstag Fire Edict," would be used to exert broad interference with the churches, including, eventually, the closing of Bonhoeffer's Preachers Seminary. This same edict allowed the establishment of concentration camps, including the future site of Bonhoeffer's execution.

Following the exclusion of Jews from civil service in April, Bonhoeffer delivered a paper for a meeting of ministers that gained publication in June. The following excerpt demonstrates how early Bonhoeffer was willing to put himself at risk with the new regime: "When the Church sees the state exercising too little or too much

law and order, it is its task not simply to bind the wounds of the victims beneath the wheel, but also to put a spoke in the wheel itself."[10]
Not without reason, some have located the source of the Bonhoeffer
chutzpah, "in the genes" as it were. Dietrich's ninety-one-year-old
grandmother Julie (née Tafel) Bonhoeffer responded to the Reich-
initiated boycott of Jewish businesses by heading straight for the
Jewish department store in Berlin where she marched calmly past
Hitler's S.A. guards and into the store to make her purchase.

By midsummer of 1933, Hitler was master of Germany. The
Lutheran Church fell quickly under his spell. The socialist party
within the church, soon known as the German Christians, won elections in July, and nominated Ludwig Müller, handpicked by Hitler, as
Reich Bishop. Bonhoeffer made his way to Gestapo headquarters for
the first time, already questioning the compatibility of loyalty to Jesus
Christ and membership in a church that, to his mind, had lapsed into
heresy.

The response of the opposition took the form of a new confession
which would set in bold relief the responsibility of the church in the
present political crisis. The product of this effort was published at the
Barmen Synod in May 1934 with Karl Barth as its principle author at
least of its final shape. The line in the sand drawn by the opponents
of Hitler's war policy and encroachments upon ecclesiastical authority
is captured in the first article of the new confession: "Jesus Christ, as
he is attested to us in Holy Scripture, is the one Word of God whom
we have to hear, and whom we have to trust and obey in life and in
death."[11] Did this statement compromise traditional Lutheran respect
for the two realms, church and state? The opposition adherents of the
Barmen Declaration, known thereafter as the Confessing Church,
thought not. In fact, Article 5 of the declaration seems designed
to make clear the affirmation of two-realm teaching by opposition

ministers. Hitler would later exploit a sentence in this article to insist that ministers keep their mouths shut regarding politics: "We reject the false doctrine that beyond its special commission the church should and could take on the nature, tasks, and dignity which belong to the state and thus become itself an organ of the state."[12]

Bonhoeffer declined a ministry post in Prussia partly because of the adoption of the Aryan clause in September. Instead, with a bad conscience, he accepted an invitation to assume pastoral duties for two small German-speaking congregations in London, where he remained until March 1935. In response to a letter from Bonhoeffer in which he tried to explain his removal to London, Barth, who is Swiss, replied from Berlin, the center of the escalating crisis: "Stop playing either Elijah under the juniper tree or Jonah under the gourd. You ought to drop all these intellectual frills and special pleadings, however interesting, and concentrate on one thing alone, that you are a German and that your Church's house is on fire, . . . you ought to return to your post on the next ship! Or, let us say, the ship after next."[13] Barth, under investigation for an extended time because of his refusal to give the Hitler salute, was finally expelled from Germany by the minister of cultural affairs in June 1935. Bonhoeffer would face another opportunity to wait out the storm, this time in America but, once again, would essentially come to share Barth's view of the matter and return. For his part, Barth would be tormented by his own sharp advice to his young colleague, realizing that he had invited Bonhoeffer to his death.[14]

Seeds of Conspiracy

The public and international scope of Bonhoeffer's opposition to Hitler increased steadily from 1935. In 1936 he is said to have claimed that anyone lacking a "red card" (demonstrating membership in the Confessing Church) cannot go to heaven and "anyone who knowingly separates himself off from the Confessing Church in Germany, separates himself off from salvation." Clearly Bonhoeffer believed that the political crisis provided the testing ground for confessional authenticity—Ye shall know them by their fruit! That Bonhoeffer would be able, from such a dangerous position of public exposure, to duck under the Nazi radar for over six years, even joining the Reich's intelligence service, is a great wonder.

Between 1935 and 1937 Bonhoeffer led the underground seminary for the Confessing Church—first at Zingst and then at Finkenwalde. This opportunity provided Bonhoeffer with something of a laboratory to experiment with his maturing ideas regarding Christian community as well as seminary education and the special needs of Christian ministers. At Finkenwalde Bonhoeffer wrote perhaps his most widely appreciated works, *Life Together* and *The Cost of Discipleship*. We will give closer attention to Bonhoeffer's experience at Finkenwalde below.

In 1936 the minister of education removed Bonhoeffer from his university teaching post. Hitler closed the seminary at Finkenwalde in 1937. In 1938 Bonhoeffer was banned from entering the city of Berlin. His father later arranged permission for visits to the family home. On March 13, Hitler's army annexed Austria.

Certainly one significant factor in Bonhoeffer's eventual participation in the conspiracy to assassinate Hitler was the Confessing Church's gradual loss of prophetic nerve. While the church maintained, at least for a time, an impressive resistance to Reich encroachments into ecclesiastical turf, Bonhoeffer grew increasingly disappointed with its feeble response to the Jewish question. In 1938 the Confessing Synod acceded to the Reich Church's call for an oath of allegiance to the Fuehrer as a birthday present following the invasion of Austria. Confessing ministers never formally acknowledged the legitimacy of conscientious objection to military service. Even the heretofore periodic objections to Gestapo infringement of church prerogatives ceased after November 9, 1938, the notorious "night of broken glass," *Kristallnacht*.

The father of seventeen-year-old Herschel Grynszpan had been among ten thousand Jews loaded onto boxcars and deported to Poland in September. On November 7 Grynszpan arrived armed at the German Embassy in Paris intending to assassinate the ambassador in response. Instead he inflicted a mortal wound upon Ernst von Rath, the third secretary at the embassy, who ironically never shared the anti-Semitic policies of the Third Reich and at the time was under Gestapo surveillance. Hitler's response, *Kristallnacht*, marked a turning point for Germany and for Bonhoeffer. The horror of that night was felt by Germany and the world. Jewish synagogues, shops, and homes burned to the ground. Many Jews—men, women, and children—were simply shot while attempting to escape the flames. One accounting has 815 shops destroyed, 171 homes destroyed, 119 synagogues set on fire, twenty thousand Jews arrested, and thirty-six deaths. Later many put the numbers much higher in each category. The anti-Semitic impulse of Nazism seemed to come into its own after that night of horror, as though a pump had been primed, and approached something of a fever pitch that continued without abatement at least until Hitler shot himself seven years later.

The seeds of conspiracy began to spring up in several quarters independently by late 1937 and especially in 1938. Bonhoeffer's exposure to one of these groups came through his brother-in-law Hans von Dohnanyi, who served as personal assistant to the minister of justice, Franz Gürtner. Dohnanyi, along with General Hans Oster, belonged to the *Abwehr* (the Intelligence Service of the OKW or High Command of the Armed Forces) and had been assigned to investigate a political crisis in the military. General Werner Freiherr von Fritsch, the natural successor to Blomberg as general field marshall, had been framed by Herrmann Goering, who coveted the position for himself. Goering, eventually named by Hitler as his successor, welcomed accusations that von Fritsch, a lifelong bachelor, was homosexual and arranged for a known informer against homosexuals who was at the time imprisoned to be brought forth to accuse von Fritsch. The investigation drew together military and political figures opposed to Hitler and gave impetus to plans for his overthrow. Because von Fritsch had been popular as army commander, would-be conspirators sought to take advantage of the opportunity to encourage hesitant enemies of the Fuehrer.

Meanwhile momentous political and military events proceeded one after the other that would plunge the world into another global war. In September 1938 at Munich, Britain and France acceded to Hitler's demand, though put forward by Mussolini, to annex the Sudetenland of Czechoslovakia. By March of the next year, Czechoslovakia ceased to exist. Also in 1938, the Godesberg Declaration legitimized the pro-Nazi "German Christians." Meanwhile Bonhoeffer agonized over an invitation by Professors Reinhold Niebuhr and Paul Lehmann to come to New York, assume a teaching appointment at Union Seminary, and escape the dangerous political situation in his homeland. In June 1939, with an uneasy conscience, Bonhoeffer, along with his brother Karl-Friedrich, boarded the *Bremen* and made the voyage across the Atlantic.

Cut off from news of events in Germany, Bonhoeffer found New York increasingly intolerable, as the following diary entries make plain:

JUNE 13

The first lonely hours are difficult. I do not know why I am
here, whether it is wise, whether the result will be worth-
while. . . . Now almost a fortnight has gone without my
knowing what is happening there. It is almost unbearable.

JUNE 14

Prayers. The short prayer—the whole family kneels down—
in which we remembered the German brethren, almost
overwhelmed me.

JUNE 15

My thoughts about Germany have not left me since yesterday evening. I should not have thought it possible for anyone of my age, after so many years abroad, to be so terribly
homesick. . . . This inactivity, or activity as the case may
be, really become simply unbearable to us when we think
of the brethren and the precious time. The whole weight of
self-reproach because of a wrong decision comes back and
almost chokes me.[15]

On June 20 he wandered aimlessly in Times Square, giving free reign
to his tortured thoughts until, at length, he decided to return. He tried
to explain his decision to Niebuhr:

It was a mistake for me to come to America. . . . I will have
no right to participate in the reconstruction of Germany
after the war if I do not share the tribulations of this time
with my people. . . . Christians in Germany are faced with
the fearful alternatives either of willing their country's
defeat so that Christian civilization may survive, or of

willing its victory and destroying our civilization. I know which of the two alternatives I have to choose but I cannot make the choice from a position of safety.

No doubt Bonhoeffer could have both served the church and spoken out politically in remarkable and useful ways from the safety open to him outside Germany. That he chose not to do so exposes something essential for any accurate understanding and assessment of Bonhoeffer's life and work. Interpretation of famously enigmatic concepts which would surface in Bonhoeffer's writings such as "religionless Christianity" or "worldly Christianity" would profit from beginning here, with this fateful decision. Risky, self-sacrificing service to the church and to the world, in the name of Jesus Christ, belongs organically to Christian obedience. In his own words from *The Cost of Discipleship*:

> When Christ calls a man, he bids him come and die. Not in pursuit of something for oneself. All things are ours already in Jesus. Not in order to make something of oneself. Our lives are hidden with Christ in God. Rather, in order to serve, in order to help others, in the name of Jesus Christ. Followers of Jesus are free for such service and such service belongs to and authenticates genuine witness to their crucified and risen Savior.

Why did Bonhoeffer return to Germany? At the most basic level, his answer was, "Because I am a German and a Christian."

Bonhoeffer took up his previous work among the congregations first in Pomerania—the sandy, lake-strewn hinterland of present-day northwestern Poland—and later among the parishes of East Prussia. In January 1940, the Gestapo closed the collective pastorates in Gross-Schlönwitz and Köslin, which were actually disguised seminaries. After Dunkirk fell on June 5, 1940, German divisions swarmed across France like a tidal wave. The swastika was hoisted on the Eiffel Tower on June 14. France surrendered three days later. On that day Bonhoeffer and his close friend and eventual biographer, Eberhard Bethge, were enjoying the sun at Memel on the Baltic Sea at an open-air café when the news came over a loudspeaker. German patrons stood on their chairs and sang *"Deutschland, Deutschland, über alles"* (Germany! Germany! over all!). Bonhoeffer stood and raised his arm in the standard Hitler salute while Eberhard sat and stared. Bonhoeffer insisted, "Raise your arm! Are you crazy?" Later he whispered, "We shall have to run risks for very different things now, but not for that salute!"[16]

Soon afterwards the Gestapo raided a Bible study Bonhoeffer was leading near Köinigsberg, after which Bonhoeffer was labeled a subversive and banned from public speaking. The Pomeranian police put him under immediate and smothering surveillance, requiring Bonhoeffer to report frequently on his movements. On September 4, Admiral Wilhelm Canaris, head of the Intelligence Service (*Abwehr*), at the urging of Oster and Dohnanyi, declared Bonhoeffer indispensable to its work owing to his frequent travels along the eastern front. He was stationed at Munich, far from the Pomeranian police. Bonhoeffer took refuge in the Benedictine monastery at Ettal, began work on his *Ethics*, and awaited his first assignment as an intelligence officer. Bonhoeffer now burned the candle at both ends, as the saying goes, living a double life as pastor and underground political operative.

By July Germany had invaded Denmark, Norway, Holland, Belgium, Luxembourg, and France. In August the Luftwaffe began relentless bombing of London. Hitler had been right and the key figures of the resistance movement had been wrong in their estimate of the enemies of the Third Reich, at least until the American and British forces landed at Normandy on D-Day. Until then Hitler's defeat appeared, at ante, in the West, increasingly difficult to imagine. From 1940 to 1943 Bonhoeffer alternated between a life of extreme tension and surreal luxury as he embraced the life of pastor and counterespionage agent—traveling widely and in high style as a member of the *Abwehr*, leading Bible studies in remote villages, and, eventually, plotting the assassination of Adolf Hitler.

Between the fall of France in 1940 and the German offensive against Russia in June 1941, Bonhoeffer worked to restore relationships between the German resistance and contacts among the Allies. The chief objective was to secure commitments by the Allies to treat a non-Nazi Germany on honorable terms in a postwar era should the conspirators succeed in deposing Hitler, whether by arrest or by assassination. His trip to Switzerland in February seemed fruitful at the time, not least because it afforded the opportunity to assure former friends in the ecumenical community that the resistance still existed and if anything had stiffened in resolve. Erwin Sutz, who entertained Bonhoeffer in Raperswil, reported Bonhoeffer insisting, "You can rely on it, we shall overthrow Hitler!"[17] W. A. Visser'Hooft, provisional secretary of the World Council of Churches, was likewise reassured by Bonhoeffer's visit. In a letter to Bishop Bell, he writes, "Many of [the Germans] have really the same reaction to all that has happened and is happening as you or as I have."[18]

Two communications from the National Office for Literature (*Richsschrifttumskammer*) awaited his return from Switzerland. Dated March 17 and 19 respectively, the first levied a fine for not applying for certification as a writer. The second letter forbade Bonhoeffer's supposed application on the grounds that he had already suffered the ban against public speaking for "subversive activity." The *Abwehr* viewed one administrative department of the Reich acting against another as too common to merit response. Later this nonchalance would be cited against Bonhoeffer by Gestapo interrogators.

Between March and June optimism grew among the conspirators in the wake of Hitler's March 30 Commissar Order. Soviet military units included commissars charged with nurturing, monitoring, and enforcing Communist party loyalty. Hitler's order required the immediate liquidation of commissars falling into the hands of German units. Such indefensibly criminal lunacy threatened to drag the German military down into the muck of the murderous SS. Even Rudolf Hess, "the Fuehrer's representative," flew to Great Britain in an abortive attempt to initiate talks to end the war. The ranks of the conspirators grew and old-timers took heart. Such hopefulness proved too short-lived. Hitler invaded the Soviet Union on June 22, and initial victories solidified his position.

In hindsight, Hitler's invasion of the Soviet Union actually proved to mark the beginning of the end for the Third Reich. Stalin, taken by surprise, had continued to ship raw materials to the Nazi regime up to the last moment. Would Hitler succeed where Napoleon had failed? In spite of popular abhorrence for Stalin in the United States, they preferred temporary embrace of the Soviets to defeat at the hands of Hitler. Even Churchill, with his fierce anticommunism unabated, was prepared to acknowledge any foe of Hitler as his ally and said as much with characteristic flair: "If Hitler invaded Hell, I would make at least a favorable reference to the Devil in the House of Commons."[19] On August 14, Roosevelt and Churchill signed the Atlantic Charter off the coast of Newfoundland, renouncing desire for new territories, affirming the rights of peoples to choose their own governments and calling for the disarmament of aggressor nations after the destruction of the Nazis. Hitler and his pumped-up war machine barely took note of the charter, but around the world hope was kindled at the renewed resolve of the two great Western powers.

During the spring and summer of 1941, the conspiring segment of the opposition met frequently, sometimes at the home of Rüdiger Schleicher, other times at the home of Dietrich's brother Klaus. Time after time they bolstered themselves with the conviction that, by some certain date, Hitler's risky self-destructive insanity would precipitate his demise, only to be disappointed. Still the group repeatedly stirred itself to renewed hope, often with the help of Bonhoeffer, who later wrote of the crucial role of optimism under such trying circumstances:

> The essence of optimism is not its view of the present, but the fact that it is the inspiration of life and hope when others give in; it enables a man to hold his head high when everything seems to be going wrong; it gives him strength to sustain reverses and yet to claim the future for himself instead of abandoning it to his opponent . . . the optimism that is will for the future should never be despised, even if it is proved wrong a hundred times.[20]

Opposition efforts continued along two tracks. First, and with each passing month more predominant, was the conspiracy to depose Hitler by whatever means. Still, efforts to shape peace terms favorable to Germany in a postwar context also claimed their attention. Bonhoeffer once again traveled to Switzerland in autumn; this time not only to gather information from friends among the Allies but also to press for consideration of the postwar peace and to argue against the wisdom of a too-simple identification of Germany with Hitler and the Third Reich even from the Allied standpoint. The prevailing attitude toward such ideas in London seemed to be utter disinterest. Understandably, victory and disarmament animated Churchill's thinking and tended to edge out other concerns. The formal announcement of the Allied demand for "unconditional surrender" would not come until January 1943 when Roosevelt and Churchill met at Casablanca, but the policy itself had taken root at least as early as the fall of France.

True to his "doctrine of optimism," Bonhoeffer returned home in late September brimming with hope only to confront the newly decreed requirement that all Jews display the pernicious yellow star, which would soon facilitate their massive deportation to the concentration camps and death chambers. Under interrogation in 1944, Bonhoeffer would be reminded that people donning the star had been seen entering the two-family homes in Berlin during those early days. In the succeeding months, what one previously heard of from Poland and other occupied areas now occurred right before one's eyes in Munich, Hamburg, and Berlin itself. Families were snatched away in the night. Whole Jewish communities marched into the neighborhood synagogue on false pretenses only to be dispatched to Auschwitz and Auschwitz II (Birkenau). Soon after his homecoming, Dietrich and his family helped their sixty-eight-year-old Jewish friend and neighbor pack for her "resettlement."

By fall of 1941, the word spread concerning the so-called "final solution" of the Jewish problem, which meant simply, their liquidation. Admiral Canaris along with Bonhoeffer, Karl Barth, and others launched Operation 7 by which the machinery of the *Abwehr* facilitated the smuggling of Jews to the West. In October the conspiracy gained unexpected impetus when longtime Hitler adversary Dr. Fabian von Schlabrendorff appeared from the eastern front with news that interference by Hitler and the SS with the Army had inclined some to entertain a *Putsch* against the regime. Even army commander Brauchitsch left the door open for such considerations. This was the vital link missing between the Berlin conspirators and forces capable of deploying military units should Hitler be over-thrown. Intense preparations proceeded apace until the bombshell came on December 19; Hitler forced Brauchitsch's retirement and named himself commander in chief of the army.

During the following weeks the conspirators accepted for the first time that the *sine qua non* of the *Putsch* must include, and indeed begin, with Hitler's assassination. Once this realization became clear, Bonhoeffer, knowing nothing about the handling of guns or explosives, let it be known that, if, in the end, the deed fell to him, he was ready to carry it out. Urgency settled upon the conspirators, and their lives became a self-conscious race between assassination and their own arrest. Bonhoeffer responded to the new realities with both realism and hope as he prepared his will and announced his engagement to marry.

Bonhoeffer had first become acquainted with Maria von Wedemeyer, eighteen years his junior, while leading the seminary at Finkenwalde. Maria's parents and her grandmother, Ruth von Kleist-Retzow, had been among the many patrons supporting the work in Pomerania and had arranged for some of their young ones to attend services at the seminary. Bonhoeffer had even been asked to prepare a select group of children for confirmation, including Maria's brother Max. The von Wedemeyers and von Kleist-Retzows belonged to the landed aristocracy of Pomerania and exposed Bonhoeffer to, among other things, the special difference a believing father can make within the family clan. Hans, Maria's father, who had taken special interest in his son's confirmation, fell on the eastern front in August 1942, affecting Bonhoeffer deeply.

In November Bonhoeffer visited Frau von Wedemeyer to ask for permission to marry her daughter Maria, the third of seven children. Still adjusting to the tragic loss of her husband, she received the request with not a little hesitance and some anxiety, not only because of the age difference involved but also because of the mysterious and seemingly dangerous nature of Bonhoeffer's work. Much to his dismay, Frau von Wedemeyer suggested that Dietrich and Maria stay apart for one year and revisit the matter after the separation. But, alas, she relented, and the engagement took place on January 17, 1943, with an agreement to delay its public announcement for some time. At length the announcement was precipitated not according to the original arrangements but by Bonhoeffer's arrest and imprisonment in April of the same year.

By the early summer of 1942, both Dohnanyi and Bonhoeffer had been warned that they were under Gestapo surveillance involving wiretaps and the interception of mail. Ironically this invasion had not been prompted by their conspiratorial activities but by a wholly unrelated Reich push for efficiency between the military and *Abwehr*.

The most reliable and hopeful contact in the west, Bishop Bell, was to be in Sweden for a time in the spring of 1942. Bonhoeffer boarded a plane for Stockholm in a last desperate attempt to secure assurances from the Allies, particularly Britain, to give a provisional German government time to prove its good intentions should Hitler's overthrow be achieved. In the weeks and months following his meetings with Bonhoeffer, Bell expended himself heroically in meetings, conferences, speeches, and publications in an attempt to advance the aims of the conspirators. The crucial assurance sought by Bell and the resistance was an unambiguous Allied distinction between Hitler and Germany. Just this distinction had been broadcast into Germany by the BBC in July. Bell pressed. Remarkably the question of the distinction was put on the schedule for the Upper House of Parliament for the December 9 session. Just before this session the matter was postponed to give Foreign Minister Anthony Eden an opportunity to meet with Bell and explain why the BBC broadcast, meant only for German ears, must be left out of any parliamentary discussion. Instead Eden suggested a link between the policy and a November 6 speech by Stalin in which the proposed distinction was sharply drawn. After considerable struggle and further scheduling and postponement, Bell raised his question on March 10, 1943. The government spokesman's response seemed to confirm the distinction between Hitler and Germany as official policy of Britain: "I now say in plain terms, on behalf of His Majesty's government that we agree with Premier Stalin, first that the Hitlerite State should be destroyed and secondly, that the whole German people is not, as Dr. Goebbels has been trying to persuade them, thereby doomed to destruction."[21]

Schlabrendorff planted his British-made, nonhissing bomb on March 13. Fellow conspirator Major General Henning von Tresckow had preferred to have Hitler "mowed down" upon arrival at headquarters on that day, but the needed order from the field marshall was not obtained. Never mind, "the semblance of an accident," Schlabrendorff reasoned, "would avoid the political disadvantages of a murder."[22] Schlabrendorff combined two explosive packets in one parcel resembling a couple of brandy bottles. Tresckow had asked Army General Staff Colonel Heinz Brandt if he would be so kind as to deliver "the brandy" to his friend General Stieff who would accompany Hitler on a flight from Smolensk to East Prussia. Schlabrendorff stood holding the parcel that day at the airfield, reached inside to trigger the timing mechanism, and handed Brandt the brandy bomb.

The bomb was set to explode over Minsk. Bonhoeffer along with Dohnanyi and their conspirator friends listened anxiously in Berlin for news of the plane crash. It never came. Instead, two hours after the expected explosion, a routine announcement that Hitler had landed at Rastenburg near Smolensk came across the wire. Miraculously the bomb went undiscovered. Questioned by Tresckow about the package, Brandt responded that he had forgotten to deliver the package! Tresckow insisted that the original parcel not be delivered. Alas, a mistake had been made. Schlabrendorff, with extraordinary courage, made his way to Hitler's headquarters and exchanged the bomb for real brandy this time. Schlabrendorff remembered the event: "I can still recall my horror when Brandt handed me the bomb and gave it a jerk that made me fear a belated explosion. Feigning a composure I did not feel I took the bomb, immediately got into a car, and drove to the neighboring railway junction of Korschen."[23]

The disappointment failed to weaken the conspirators' determination. Hitler was to attend the Heroes' Memorial Day Ceremonies, accompanied by Goering, Himmler, and Keitel on March 21. Hitler and his entourage were set to spend a half hour viewing an exhibit of Russian war trophies arranged by Major von Gersdorff, a fellow conspirator. This meant that a bomb could take out top leaders of the Third Reich along with Hitler, but the attempt would have to be a suicide mission. Gersdorff volunteered to blow himself to bits for the cause. But it was not to be. Frigid weather meant that the normally ten-minute fuses might require as much as twelve minutes or more to detonate the bomb. In keeping with his vigilant security precautions, Hitler made a last-minute change, allowing only eight minutes, not thirty, for the exhibition. The assassination attempt was scrapped.

On Sunday afternoon, Rüdiger Schleicher hosted a rehearsal for the upcoming seventy-fifth birthday celebration cantata for Dietrich's father Karl. The concentration of accomplished musicians and grandchildren resulted in a veritable concert with Klaus on the cello, Schleicher on the violin, and Dietrich at the piano. Once again news of Hitler's death never came. Two weeks later Bonhoeffer and Dohnanyi were arrested, and Oster was banned from the *Abwehr*.

Arrest

Ironically the arrests had nothing to do with the conspiracy to assassinate Hitler but with a long-standing internal Reich struggle to curtail the relative independence of the *Abwehr* under the guise of reforms designed to improve efficiency. Consul Schmidhuber, once active among the resistance, had been arrested in October 1942 in connection with the Gestapo investigation of the *Abwehr*. Schmidhuber had been one of Bonhoeffer's superiors at the Munich office and knew of the Operation 7 efforts to smuggle Jews into Switzerland. Under interrogation Bonhoeffer's name had surfaced and led to the wiretapping and monitoring initiated as early as late spring of 1942.

An unknown male voice answered Bonhoeffer's call to his sister Christine von Dohnanyi on April 5, 1943. Convinced a search of the Dohnanyi house was underway and that his own arrest was imminent, he crossed to the house of his sister Ursula Schleicher and had a robust meal prepared in anticipation of a Gestapo-imposed fast to come. At midday a black Mercedes stopped in front of the Bonhoeffer residence in the cul-de-sac in Marienburger Alle. Soon Karl brought the news to his son Dietrich at the Schleicher home that two men wished to speak with him. Gestapo operatives Judge Advocate Dr. Manfred Roeder and Detective Sondregger drove Bonhoeffer away. He never saw Marienburger Alle again.

Prison

Courage is not the absence of fear but the will to act in the face of fear. Such was the character of Bonhoeffer's courage. Strong as he was mentally, emotionally, and physically, he cringed at the prospect of deprivation, interrogation or, God forbid, torture. He was sure he would not hold up well. On a scrap of paper salvaged from his early days of solitary confinement in Tegel prison, we find these words: "Suicide, not because of consciousness of guilt but because basically I am already dead, draw a line, summing up."[24] *Could suicide become a duty where the danger of betraying others threatened?* Bonhoeffer wondered. In fact, he did hold up under interrogation, faithfully repeating all that he and Dohnanyi had rehearsed for just such circumstances.

Bonhoeffer's extensive notes along with some official minutes from the hearings survive. Enquiries included Bonhoeffer's exemption from military service, Operation 7, his international travel, and his employment of the *Abwehr* in the aid of the Confessing Church. Yet there seemed to be little of substance to be found. Nothing emerged to tie Bonhoeffer to conspiracy. Bonhoeffer even referred his interrogators to his own published writings: "If anyone wants to learn something of my conception of the duty of Christian obedience towards the authorities, he should read my exposition of Romans 13 in my book *The Cost of Discipleship.* The appeal to subjection to the will and the demands of authority for the sake of Christian conscience has probably seldom been expressed more strongly than there."[25]

Once the period of interrogation ended in July, he set up his cell as a study and began to reacquaint himself with the old pursuits of his ministry days, though he would not settle down to study and writing in earnest for another year. Equally costly to Bonhoeffer upon entering the conspiracy was the conviction that he would no longer be qualified to preach and teach as the clergyman he once hoped to become. That he continued to wrestle with such notions, not only as far as the church was concerned, but generally, is confirmed in a collection of essays found hidden in his attic, dedicated to his fellow conspirators for Christmas 1942: "We have been silent witnesses of evil deeds. We have been drenched by many storms. We have learnt the arts of equivocation and pretense. Experience has made us suspicious of others, and kept us from being truthful and open. Intolerable conflicts have worn us down and even made us cynical. Are we still of any use?"[26]

Bound hand and foot, Bonhoeffer was eventually settled into Cell No. 92 on the first floor rather than the third to shield the potentially valuable witness from the danger of bomb attacks. The solitary confinement was exacerbated by an order forbidding the guards from conversing with the new prisoner. Eventually though, these restrictions would be lifted, and Bonhoeffer would receive comparatively soft treatment once word spread that he was indeed of the famous Berlin Bonhoeffer family.

Soon it became clear that Bonhoeffer's hopes for trial and acquittal were almost entirely bound up with the fate of his lawyer, brother-in-law, and coconspirator, Hans von Dohnanyi. Through frequent visits from family, friends, and his fiancée, and use of code language, Bonhoeffer was able to follow the developments in Dohnanyi's trial closely. Both Bonhoeffer and Dohnanyi were interrogated by the Nazi judge advocate, Manfred Roeder, who had driven the Mercedes to Marienburger Alle on that fateful April afternoon. An ambitious lawyer belonging to the *Luftwaffe*, Roeder was famous for securing three death sentences in the sensational *Rote Kapelle* trials of 1942. A titanic mental battle ensued between the two lawyers, with Roeder bent on securing a conviction for high treason. Bonhoeffer's trial could not go forward apart from the resolution of Dohnanyi's case. Dohnanyi got the better of Roeder, and on July 23, 1943, the pursuit of the high treason charge was abandoned in favor of lesser infractions. Roeder was eventually removed from the case by "promotion" and was replaced in February 1944. Still Dohnanyi's trial continued, leaving Bonhoeffer to watch and wait. Dohnanyi became gravely ill. The Gestapo took full control of his case in July 1944, and Dohnanyi was transferred to the concentration camp Sachsenhausen where he was able for a time to use his illness as a tactic of delay in his trial.

Bonhoeffer's own trial suffered from a repeated setting of dates and postponements. From April 1944, Bonhoeffer settled down with his books and his writing, producing significant portions of his posthumous *Ethics* and the whole of *Widerstand und Eergebung* (Resistance and Submission), published in English as *Letters and Papers from Prison*. These writings offer extraordinary insights into the struggle for a good conscience by a committed follower of Christ caught up in the whirlwind that was the rise and fall of the Third Reich.

Hopes Dashed

After eight months of incarceration, Bonhoeffer wrote to his friend Eberhard Bethge:

> I want to assure you that I haven't for a moment regretted coming back in 1939—nor any of the consequences either. I knew quite well what I was doing, and I acted with a clear conscience. I have no wish to cross out of my life anything that has happened since, either to me personally (would I have got engaged otherwise?) . . . I regard my being kept here (do you remember that I prophesied to you last March about what the year would bring?) as being involved in the fate of Germany in which I was determined to share.[27]

Fourteen months had passed since Bonhoeffer's arrest when, on June 6, 1944, British and American troops, carried by a thousand ships, landed at Omaha Beach on the Normandy coast between the rivers Vire and Orne. Idiotic orders from Hitler prevented the swift deployment of Panzer (tank) divisions needed to repel the invading Allies. German defenses collapsed on the western front in the face of superior air and naval bombardment. Hitler slept while his generals begged in vain for permission to release their tanks. On June 20 the long-delayed Russian offensive from the east commenced, essentially sealing the fate of Nazi Germany.

These developments fatally undermined the hopes of the conspirators against Hitler. General Field Marshal Rommel, though opposed to the assassination plot, remained crucial to the conspirators' post-assassination plans, both because of his high rank and his daring personality. In a July 15 letter to the Fuehrer, Rommel all but insisted upon German surrender, telling General Speidel, "I have given him his last chance . . . if he does not take it, we will act."[28] Two days later, while making his way from the western front to headquarters, low-flying Allied fighter planes shot up Rommel's car near Livarot, leaving the field marshal critically wounded and useless to the conspiracy. Only the rapid replacement of the Nazi regime following Hitler's assassination, prior to the simultaneous Allied assaults from east and west, could possibly secure favorable terms for a postwar Germany. An imploding German army, retreating from both fronts, could expect little mercy from the freshly exultant enemy hungry for victory.

The linchpin of the final assassination attempt was the selection of the assassin himself—Lieutenant Colonel Klaus Philip Schenk, Count von Stauffenberg. In April 1943 Stauffenberg had suffered what, for most men, would have been career-ending injuries when his car drove into a minefield. Despite losing his left eye, right hand, two fingers of the other hand, and suffering injuries to his left ear and knee, by midsummer he was demanding reinstatement to active duty. The long convalescence had only strengthened his conviction that the assassination of Adolf Hitler was a sacred mission.

At the end of June, the conspirators celebrated unexpected good news when Stauffenberg was promoted to full colonel and appointed chief of staff to General Fromm, commander of the home army. Now subject to frequent summons to Hitler's office, Stauffenberg laid plans for the planting of yet another bomb. And since Fromm could not be definitely counted on, Stauffenberg would have to direct the army to secure Berlin immediately following the assassination. The first opportunity came on July 11 at Obersalzberg at a meeting set to include Himmler and Goering as well as Hitler. When Himmler did not show, Stauffenberg rang General Olbricht in Berlin, who urged him to wait for another attempt on the triumvirate. On July 15, Stauffenberg left the bomb-bearing briefcase with Hitler to phone Olbricht and declare his intention to detonate the explosive, only to return and find Hitler gone.

On July 20, Stauffenberg, summoned to meet with Hitler at the so-called "Wolf's Lair" at Rastenburg in East Prussia, made his way past the guards once again toward the Fuehrer with a time bomb in tow. At around 12:30, having broken the capsule of the timing device, leaving ten minutes before detonation, Stauffenberg was invited into Hitler's conference room occupied by about twenty persons with Hitler seated at the table. Goering and Himmler were not present. Having taken his chair, Stauffenberg slid the bomb-bearing briefcase toward Hitler, but still it bulged outward from the table. Still it was clearly close enough to kill him, especially since it leaned against the inside of a stout oak support of the table facing Hitler. When Stauffenberg managed to absent himself briefly under the ruse of a telephone call, Colonel Brandt moved the briefcase to the other side of the support in order to gain a closer view of the map laid out on the table.

Keitel, annoyed that Stauffenberg was not poised to give his report, stepped outside the conference room only to be told that the newly promoted chief of staff had hurriedly left the building upon exiting the meeting. Keitel reentered the conference room at 12:42.

The bomb exploded. Stauffenberg, stationed a couple hundred yards away, eyes fixed on the buildings, saw the bodies hurtle through the windows at the blast. He had no doubt that none had survived. Keitel escaped uninjured and Hitler, only shaken, was probably saved by the innocent and unwitting Brandt who had shifted the briefcase a few inches.

For an entire year Bonhoeffer believed in the likelihood of his acquittal at trial followed by release from prison. Such hope ended abruptly on July 20, 1944, with Stauffenberg's failed attempt on Hitler. Bonhoeffer also knew that his own fate was now sealed.

Bonhoeffer devised but then abandoned a plan for escape in fear that success would provoke Gestapo action against his family and friends. On Sunday, October 8, Bonhoeffer was transferred to the underground prison at Prinz-Albrecht-Strasse. By February 1945, five members of Bonhoeffer's family were in Gestapo custody. Death sentences were handed down for his brother Klaus and Rüdiger Schleicher. Bonhoeffer was secretly moved to Berlin where he withstood four months of interrogation. After this he spent seven weeks at an air-raid shelter in the concentration camp at Buchenwald before being moved again, this time to Flossenbürg. At Hitler's midday conference on April 5, it was decided that members of the so-called "Zossen group" in which Bonhoeffer was included, would be executed. Bonhoeffer had inadvertently been placed on a transport and had to be brought back to Flossenbürg, He arrived late on the evening of April 8. Early the next morning Bonhoeffer and his friends were hanged.

The camp doctor recalled seeing Bonhoeffer that day:
Through the half-open door in one room of the huts I saw Pastor Bonhoeffer, before taking off his prison garb, kneeling on the floor praying fervently to his God. I was most deeply moved by the way this lovable man prayed, so devout

and so certain that God heard his prayer. At the place of
execution, he again said a short prayer and then climbed
the steps to the gallows, brave and composed. His death
ensued after a few seconds. In the almost fifty years that
I worked as a doctor, I have hardly ever seen a man die so
entirely submissive to the will of God.[29]

The bombs of the approaching Allied forces could be heard at
Flossenbürg in the days preceding the executions. Two weeks later
the American army liberated Flossenbürg, finding only two thousand
prisoners left alive. One week later, at the age of fifty-six, Hitler shot
himself in the mouth with a revolver.

Does Dietrich Bonhoeffer belong to the ranks of Christian martyrs? Does he have something to say to our generation? Bonhoeffer
not only faced the complexities and horrors at the heart of the modern world; he was a preacher and a pastor who continued to write
down his thoughts. Bonhoeffer has much to say to Bible-believing
Christians in the twenty-first century. In the chapters that follow, we
will let Bonhoeffer speak to us of the costly discipleship he pursued.
We look first for help with knowing and doing the will of God.

Chapter Two

KNOWING AND DOING THE WILL OF GOD

Do not get into the habit of interpreting Scripture in light of personal experience. Do not measure God's word. Let it measure my word, my life.

DIETRICH BONHOEFFER

Not Following One's Heart

BONHOEFFER, NO DOUBT INFLUENCED by Karl Barth, retained a robust view of sin that prevented any identification of his own intuition or interpretation of his experience with the will of God. Convictions arising from deep thought and feeling or even prayer do not guarantee truth of any kind for Bonhoeffer. The Christian comes to the Bible not to find an echo of his own convictions but to hear the voice of God. That voice is more likely to surprise and confound than to confirm any previously held convictions. To come to the Scripture as a disciple is to enter, in the words of Karl Barth, "the strange new world of the Bible."[30]

This strain of dogmatic biblicism raises the question of the role of personal experience in Bonhoeffer's thinking. There can be no doubt that in Bonhoeffer's conception of true discipleship, experience, feeling, and what might be referred to as heart religion, were not only allowed but expected and celebrated. But the word of Scripture judges all things, including insights we think we receive from other sources.

Bonhoeffer was a publishing researcher and scholar, grappling with the biblical languages and conversant with the latest approaches to biblical interpretation. Despite his surprising and certainly atypical departure from an academic trajectory in favor of hands-on ministry, Bonhoeffer continued to pursue high level studies in theology, sociology, and philosophy.

Bonhoeffer let his students labor under the exacting rigors of language study at Finkenwalde as he had in the university. Yet, during times of daily meditation, these same students were encouraged to set aside the Greek and Hebrew Scriptures in favor of the familiar Luther translation of the Bible they had known from childhood. Why? Because in meditation and prayer the whole person—mind, body, and soul—opens up to God, longing to hear his voice from the Bible. Bonhoeffer believed that the familiar, vernacular text facilitated this listening quest more effectively than could the original languages. Bonhoeffer was alert to the role of experience and the heart in true discipleship. But what was the nature of that role? What do experience and prayer have to do with seeking and finding the word and will of God? We will attempt to answer these questions in due course, but first we must explore certain transforming developments in Bonhoeffer's approach to the Bible.

Back to the Bible Movement

Though Bonhoeffer denies any radical break in his development as a theologian, he does admit to a significant change in his focus and in the clarity with which he understood his calling. According to Bonhoeffer's biographer and close friend Eberhard Bethge, those who met him after 1931 "were impressed by his breadth of knowledge, concentrated energy, analytical and critical acumen and also by a personal commitment that engaged the whole of his personality and showed itself in innumerable ways of practical behavior."[31] Attendance in worship and a systematic devotion to Bible study, prayer, and meditation on Scripture had become staples of his life.

One of Bonhoeffer's students from 1932 remembers his teacher's admonition that they "should not forget that every word of Holy Scripture was a quite personal message of God's love for us," after which he asked them whether they loved Jesus.[32] Such heart religion and simple biblicism in the context of the prevailing head-heavy German Lutheranism must have smacked of a lapse into antiintellectual Moravianism or charismatic mumbo jumbo. Only Bonhoeffer's solid academic credentials shielded him from such critiques.

Bonhoeffer identified the cause of this momentous awakening: "Then something happened, something that has changed and transformed my life to the present day. For the first time I discovered the Bible . . . . I had often preached, I had seen a great deal of the church, and talked and preached about it—but I had not yet become a Christian."[33]

A remarkable letter to his brother-in-law Rüdiger Schleicher reveals some of the changes that were taking place in Bonhoeffer's approach to the Bible. Bonhoeffer responds in part to concerns Schleicher had raised in a previous letter. At the time, Schleicher accepted the liberal, higher critical reading of Scripture then dominant in the German universities. Examples of so-called "higher critical" analysis of Scripture include source theory and form criticism. According to source theory, many Old Testament books resulted from the combining of multiple sources into a single narrative. These various sources, it was contended, were produced by separate authors or communities of faith captivated by their own immediate needs but comparatively disinterested in the historical accuracy of the documents they produced.

New Testament "form criticism" was exemplified most spectacularly in the work of Rudolf Bultmann. These thinkers claimed that the Gospels represented the work of editors who drew their material from a hypothetical document called Q and from snippets and stories regarding Jesus which had circulated for years or even decades in oral form, hence the term *form* criticism. Form critics sought to go behind the received text to the so-called original oral forms and to rearrange texts according to a supposedly more original shape.

Today fewer and fewer scholars approach the Bible according to the heady pretensions of early twentieth-century higher criticism. Evidence demonstrates that Bonhoeffer never completely rejected these and other strands of higher criticism, but he also recognized certain limitations and dangers of such high-handed critical readings of the Bible. Bonhoeffer acknowledged that the Bible could be approached like any other book, but he insisted that such readings failed to discern the true character of the Bible and thus failed to obtain its characteristic treasure, namely, the Word of the living God.

Huddle House
3150 39th St.SW
Fargo, ND 58104
701.282.7766

Server: Cassandra   DOB: 04/11/2013
01:52 PM   04/11/2013
Table 31/1   3/30058

                           SALE

M/C   3145808
Card #XXXXXXXXXXXXX0692
Magnetic card present: ALDRICH FRED
Card Entry Method: S

Approval: 049974

                              Amount: $ 7.51

                               + Tip: _____

                             = Total: ___9,_____

                  I agree to pay the above
                  total amount according to the
                  card issuer agreement.

X_____

                       Customer Copy

To Schleicher he wrote: "I want to confess quite simply that I believe the Bible alone is the answer to all our questions, and that we only need to ask persistently and with some humility in order to receive the answer from it."[34]

Bonhoeffer is not adopting an antihistorical, mystical approach to the interpretation of the Bible. Throughout his short life Bonhoeffer made use of background studies as well as grammatical and historical tools for Bible study, and he required his own students to master the skills necessary for such research. The questions of authorship, historical setting, and original audience provided crucial, even determinative, insight into the meaning of Scripture. But Bonhoeffer rejected the imposition of prior commitments and agendas upon the text, and he believed that, following rigorous study, the minister of the Word should adopt a prayerful, trusting posture before the text, opening himself to the Spirit and the Word. By contrast the higher critic stands above the Bible, passing judgment upon its contents. The disciple stands under the Bible and finds himself addressed by God in Christ through it.

The Sermon on the Mount especially captivated and then freed Bonhoeffer with its command and invitation to live before God and for others. His *Cost of Discipleship* would result from this life-changing discovery of the Bible. Bonhoeffer realized that within his social circle, including his family, the turn to the Bible in such a "fundamentalist-like" way would likely furrow brows all around. Yet this "conversion" (Bonhoeffer's biographer, Eberhard Bethge, covered these events under the heading "The theologian becomes a Christian") effected a total transformation in Bonhoeffer's ministerial identity.[35] He had found his calling. To his brother Karl-Friedrich he wrote: "It may be that in many things I may seem to you rather fanatical and crazy. I myself am sometimes afraid of this . . . . [yet] I now believe that

I know at last that I am on the right track—for the first time in my life."[36] And in April 1936 to his brother-in-law Rüdiger Schleicher, Bonhoeffer writes:

> Is it . . . intelligible to you if I say I am not at any point willing to sacrifice the Bible as this strange word of God, that on the contrary, I ask with all my strength what God is trying to say to us through it? Everything outside the Bible has grown too uncertain to me. I am afraid of running only into a divine counterpart of myself . . .
>
> Also I want to say to you quite personally that since I have learnt to read the Bible in this way . . . it becomes more marvelous to me every day. . . . You will not believe how glad one is to find one's way back to these elementary things after wandering on a lot of theological side-tracks.[37]

Such effusive proselytizing for a recovery of a pious reading of the Bible drew concern and criticism. Schleicher himself issued his own warning to his nephew.

Though Bonhoeffer never hitched his theological wagon to another's system, the shadow of Karl Barth looms large over this momentous episode in Bonhoeffer's development. Barth had previously experienced his own traumatic confrontation with "the strange new world within the Bible," and realized that theology worthy of the name could never be reducible to a projection of man's own highest hopes, dreams, and fantasies. Barth, especially in his early career, emphasized the "wholly otherness" of God. By this he meant to recover the realization that human ways and human thinking are not God's ways and God's thinking. God's Word comes to us as revelation and judgment, not as affirmation and confirmation of what we already knew from other sources.

It comes as revelation because nothing generally available to humanity reveals God truly. Only God reveals God. The truth about God must be found where and when God is pleased to have it found. And God's Word comes as judgment because it comes as Christ crucified. The cross places a question mark over everything human, calling into question and ultimately rendering a guilty verdict upon all humanity which has "gone its own way" in rebellion against the only true God.

Bonhoeffer never lost sight of the need for confessional seriousness within the church. It is no accident that the resistance movement so deeply shaped by Bonhoeffer was known as the Confessing Church. He viewed the Barmen Declaration of 1934 as an indispensable tool for both authentic Christian witness and resistance to Hitler's regime. Yet Bonhoeffer's "discovery of the Bible" also resulted in a renewed quest to hear the message of Scripture anew, unfettered by past understandings of its message however long-standing and "established" they might be. While Bonhoeffer's appreciation for the history of interpretation and the warranted wisdom of Protestant confessionalism informs his own grappling with the biblical text, he came to chafe at dogmatic adherence to received interpretations. In this Bonhoeffer reclaims the Protestant birthright of an unfettered Word, insisting on and celebrating the continuing privilege and responsibility of each generation of believers to interpret the Bible for itself, in its own time, and to test all things by Scripture, including the received tradition.

In connection with the Christian tradition, it is well-known that Bonhoeffer's trip to Rome during his student days sparked a fascination with Roman Catholicism that never left him. The Roman church's antiquity, complexity, and its unique combination of tolerance and intolerance made a lasting impression on Bonhoeffer. But Bonhoeffer's hope that the Roman Church would retain authentic

Christian character had nothing to do with such things but rather with the presence of the Scriptures within it: "It still has the Bible, and so long as it still has that we can still believe it to be a holy Christian church. For God's word shall not return to him empty (Isa. 55:11), whether it be preached in our or in the sister church."[38]

The Bible and Prayer

Discipleship means following, obeying, acting. Reduction of the Christian life to matters of sentiment or matters of the heart becomes incomprehensible in the face of biblical teaching. "When God calls a man, he bids him come and die."[39] Such words from Bonhoeffer's pen cut us to the quick because eight years after the ink hit the paper Bonhoeffer was hanged at Flossenburg. Bonhoeffer was not only a theologian of action but also a man of action, a man of courage. Any pursuit of Bible study and prayer as an escape from responsible, risky obedience in this world must be rejected as not only sub-Christian but anti-Christian. Yet Bonhoeffer cannot be understood apart from the vital refuge he persistently pursued and found in prayer and meditation on the Word of God.

Bonhoeffer's quest for the will of God drove him to the Bible and to prayer. Because Bonhoeffer expected the Bible to answer all crucial questions for the Christian and the church, he embraced a daily discipline of Bible study and meditation on the Word of God. This discipline, while in no way opposed to academic study of the Scriptures, was distinct from such scholarly analysis. Bonhoeffer never completely repudiated the higher critical study of the Bible then flourishing in German academic circles, but he did insist upon the limits of such approaches to the Word of God. Bonhoeffer conceded that the Christian believer may and perhaps should approach the Bible as any other book alongside secular academicians and unbelievers. Yet, as a believer, he must go further. With the saints across the centuries, he expects to hear the voice of the living God in the Bible. At some point the results of academic study must be, not cast aside, but made to serve their purpose for the Christian and for the church. The voice and will of God must be sought with all one's heart. In the words of the prophet, "You will seek Me and find Me when you search for Me with all your heart" (Jer. 29:13).

Bonhoeffer's yieldedness to the Bible resulted in an expansion of the notion of the will of God beyond a cut-and-dried search for answers to ethical questions. God in his Word provides not only or first of all the answers to the believer's questions, but the questions themselves. Prayer and meditation serve primarily the pursuit of the living God himself. Now God's concerns, God's values, God's purposes, God's demands, and God's promises take center stage. Reality and relevance become identical with God's own word to humanity and God's own judgment of the world. In a striking sense, for Bonhoeffer, as for Karl Barth before him, reality is defined by, even equated with, God's view of all things as revealed in Holy Scripture and supremely in the crucified and risen Christ. There is no reality apart from Jesus Christ. "The place where the answer is given, both to the question concerning the reality of God and to the question concerning the reality of the world, is designated solely and alone by the name Jesus Christ" (E, 192).[40] In him all things consist (Col. 1:17). Through the witness of Holy Scripture, Bonhoeffer found himself drawn into a whole world, the real world, or in the words of Karl Barth, "the strange new world of the Bible."

Believers who meditate on Scripture in pursuit of the living God are caught up in the great sweep of God's creative and redemptive acts in history. As the objects and beneficiaries of that redemption,

Christians recognize their own stake in the great divine acts of deliverance on behalf of his people in the past. They fall under God's insistence that these great acts be remembered and recognized as windows into the character and purposes of the living God.

Obsession with the Will of God

Gerhard Jacobi correctly identifies the persistent obsession driving Bonhoeffer's thinking:

At meetings of Pastors [Bonhoeffer] spoke only briefly. Twice he quoted to them nothing but the words: "one man asks: What is to come? The other: What is right? And there is the difference between the free man and the slave." He said nothing more, but those few words spoken in calmness and certainty, and out of personal freedom, found their mark. . . . He was haunted by the question about the will of God *hic and nunc* [here and now].[41]

How could a theologian and minister fixated upon ethics view the question "What is right?" as the mark of unbelieving slavery? One problem for Bonhoeffer was the latent self-centeredness he detected in such questions. He writes in *Ethics*:

Whoever wishes to take up the problem of a Christian ethic must be confronted at once with a demand which is quite without parallel. He must from the outset discard as irrelevant the two questions which alone impel him to concern himself with the problem of ethics, "How can I be good?" and "How can I do good?", and instead of these he must ask the utterly and totally different question "What is the will of God?"[42]

Where concern for one's own goodness preoccupies the mind of the disciple, justification by faith and the finished atoning work of Christ on the cross have been set aside, and a new works righteousness threatens.

If Bonhoeffer is right, it would seem that much effort and anxiety is misdirected and misspent by would-be followers of Jesus. "Attempts to identify, track, measure, evaluate, and, perhaps especially, to declare the goodness of my actions appear at least unnecessary and irrelevant if not counterproductive in face of the cross, forgiveness, and the promises of God."

The Realization of Reality

This odd, seemingly redundant phrase, "the realization of reality," is crucial to our understanding of Bonhoeffer's ethic and, thus, his conception of the will of God. It points first of all to Bonhoeffer's profound sense of God's providential ruling presence in the world here and now. When Bonhoeffer lays responsibility for shaping the future upon Christians and the church, it is not because he doubts God's power and intention to fulfill his own purposes in the future but because of his certainty that God will do so. Certainty and hope must and may characterize the believer's anticipation of the future precisely because God has bound himself to his promises. Our confidence in his promise frees us to participate in God's own work, first as witnesses to Jesus Christ and then as his disciples in the world. For Bonhoeffer, following Jesus involves the realization of reality.

What is reality? Reality is what God says it is. Reality is what God makes it to be. In Scripture we are confronted with what God has said, done, and promised to do. God's activity, speech, and promises trump and displace rival interpretations of reality. God determines the meaning of everything, period.

What is the realization of reality? It means yielding to the truth. It means reflecting in one's own life the revelation of God in Jesus Christ. Walking by faith means trusting God's revelation of reality against all supposed evidence to the contrary.

No to Situation Ethics

Though Bonhoeffer intends to base his ethic on the notion of reality, he identifies and rejects a particular unchristian reality-based ethics. Such ethics eliminate all standards and norms in favor of an examination of so-called "reality" which, according to Bonhoeffer, surrenders to "the contingent, the casual, the adventitious and the momentarily expedient."[43] Situation ethics of this type depend on sanguine, innocuous assessments of human nature incompatible with Bonhoeffer's reading of the Bible. Bonhoeffer accepts the Reformation insistence that the fall of humanity into sin resulted not only in catastrophic moral debilitation but also in so-called "noetic" effects. Without the enlightenment of the Holy Spirit, we cannot see the truth of God revealed in Jesus Christ, much less reality as established in Christ, and so recognize and traverse the moral terrain as transformed by that reality.

Doing the Will of God

Bonhoeffer believed that Christians could move into the future with boldness and even optimism born of hope and participate responsibly in the shaping of the future in accordance with God's will. In what follows, these three significant terms—boldness, optimism, and hope—indicate crucial dimensions of Bonhoeffer's ethical thinking.

Bonhoeffer was obsessed with the desire to know and to do the will of God. He embraced both the burden and the exhilaration of the Christian's happy duty to obey God's will today, in this time, in ways demanded by one's concrete, real-life situation. And yet, amazingly, Bonhoeffer also believed obedience must typically proceed without claims to direct access to the mind of God. Bonhoeffer rejected the notion that believers must or even should expect and thus wait until the claim of special revelation could be advanced to defend the final shape of one's action. There was a freedom before God to do one's best, in humility, without making extraordinary claims of certainty or special knowledge. Bonhoeffer did expect obedience to proceed with a particular certainty but not that of the illuminists from whom one hears, "God is leading me to . . ." or worse, "God has told me. . . ." The certainty Bonhoeffer sought for himself and expected within the church was one of intention and biblical faithfulness to the revelation of God in Jesus Christ and him crucified. The Christian must intend to follow the path of the cross set out in Holy Scripture.

Christian action could be scrutinized with reference to the Bible and especially in its compatibility with the revelation of God's will in Jesus Christ. Moral absolutes held little attraction for Bonhoeffer, but "following Christ" was absolutely necessary. God in Christ came to serve, came to seek and save that which was lost, and did so by allowing himself to be pushed out of the world onto the cross where he was crucified and on the third day rose from the dead. These things are not cloudy but clear and provide abundant guidance for Christian decision making.

Bethge remembers Bonhoeffer as scrupulously slow in coming to decision but also as bold and free once a decision was made. "Once the decision was taken it was neither regretted nor ever questioned."[44] In his prison poem "Stations on the Way to Freedom," Bonhoeffer insisted, "Make up your mind and come out into the tempest of living."[45] Bonhoeffer warned against hasty decisions and even insisted that the status quo has precedence over change, but the greater danger he identified was paralysis. The indefinite postponement of decision could indicate false assumptions regarding special revelation or other longings for explicit guidance. Bonhoeffer recognized the paralyzing danger of a distortive discernment fixated view of the Christian life.

Bonhoeffer believed in the seeking and receiving of divine guidance for daily living but only as a product of meditation on the Word of God. He recognized the place of, in the words of J. I. Packer, "the world of internal promptings and nudges," but only as initiated, shaped, and interpreted in the light of Scripture.[46]

No to Casuistry

Along with situation ethics Bonhoeffer also rejected another major movement and style of ethical argumentation—casuistry. The word *casuistry* derives from the Latin *casus* meaning "case" and has reference to a given *casus conscientiae* (case of conscience). Generally speaking, a casuistic ethic seeks to resolve particular cases of conscience based on general ethical principles. The casuistic moralist or counselor uses general principles as tools in order to offer instruction as to the good or evil of some past or intended action.

Typically the general principles used by casuists are drawn from three sources: the Bible, natural law, and tradition. Casuistic patterns of ethical instruction surfaced prior to the coming of Christ in rabbinical Judaism where questions of cultic law predominated. Christian casuistry appears toward the end of the first century, coinciding with a waning of confidence in the Holy Spirit as guide and lawgiver. In the writings of the early church fathers, Tertullian (c. 160–c. 225) and

Ambrose (c. 339–97), the casuistic tendency to treat the Old and New Testaments as a new law supplemented by insight from Stoic moralists is unmistakable. The increasingly formalized practice of confession during the Middle Ages understandably highlighted the attractiveness of casuistic instruction. Massive collections of moral decisions called penitentiaries were produced and used by confessors to instruct penitents mired in their own particular cases of conscience.

The Protestant Reformation of the sixteenth century marked the beginning of serious questioning and sometimes rejection of casuistry not least because of the conviction that Scripture ought not to share the spotlight with tradition, philosophy, or natural law in questions of ethics. Luther's notion of the freedom of the Christian seemed to rule out compatibility between casuistry and the gospel of Jesus Christ. John Calvin insisted that casuistic instruction usurps the role of God as the only lawgiver and ruler of souls.

Nevertheless casuistry gained a foothold in the thinking of certain Puritan divines, notably William Perkins, whose book *Concerning Cases of Conscience* bears more than passing resemblance to the medieval and Jesuit "penitentiaries" themselves. Casuistic approaches to ethical instruction were largely eclipsed in seventeenth-century Pietism, being displaced by an emphasis on the purity of intention in ethical decision rather than the actions themselves.

Before we explore Bonhoeffer's reasons for rejecting casuistry, we should pause and consider the truly magnetic allure of casuistry for both counselor and counselee. The pastoral and especially confessional attractiveness of casuistic methods accounts for its recurring appearance among Protestants, evangelical and otherwise. Clearly the most spectacular claim and promise of casuistry is the resolution of otherwise thorny, seemingly intractable, ethical cul-de-sacs which seem to confront believers of the twenty-first century.

The casuistic moralist counselor relieves conscience-stricken confessors and seekers from further agonizing and anguish. The burden of decision making is shifted to the wise casuist. Just as an obedient child finds his conscience soothed so long as his father's wishes are satisfied and his commands obeyed, so compliant subjects of casuist counselors seek to disentangle themselves not only from guilty consciences but from second thoughts.

Casuistry promises something of a recovery of the certainty Moses must have known when commanded to take his shoes off on Mount Horeb or that Peter no doubt enjoyed when told to welcome and accompany the three men sent from Cornelius. In the face of such clear instruction, agonizing evaporates at least on the question of what must be done. Questions of right and wrong, good or evil are eclipsed. Now only obedience or disobedience awaits resolution.

Certainly one burden accepted and resolved in casuistry is thrown off in Bonhoeffer's ethics. It is the burden of a particular kind of certainty. It is the burden of having to claim God's sanction for one's actions, past or intended future ones. Bonhoeffer detected in casuistry a lapse into self-justification and so away from grace and the freedom he thought proper to Christian discipleship.

The rejection of casuistry need not imply a denial of the underlying truth assumed and confronted by such an approach. Without doubt our lives involve, moment by moment, activity and decision in which we are claimed by the divine command. Certainly God's interest and judgment penetrate to the good or bad character of both the inner motivation and the outward action of our entire lives. Casuistic warning, guidance, and comfort prove attractive not only to the troubled seeker of advice and the pastor or counselor who gives it but also to every believer who yearns to yield his entire life, body and soul, to the Lord he loves. Seen from this perspective, pursuit of casuistic certainty in cases of conscience often displays deep and genuine piety, not a quick, legalistic shortcut to some contrived clearing of the conscience. Embrace of casuistic scrutiny may and no doubt often does involve the sincere desire to bring oneself completely under the sway of God's purposes for one's life. Still, the pitfalls of casuistic ethics are also significant, such as the unjustified easing of the conscience. For Bonhoeffer perhaps the most pernicious danger of the casuistry is the abandonment of justification by faith and life lived under grace and forgiveness in favor of a cheaply constructed platform for self-confidence and counterfeit certainty.

No to Immediacy

The daily quest for special, direct, individual guidance has come to dominate at least the style if not the thinking of large parts of the evangelical world. Assuming the posture of receptor of divine guidance has virtually come to define discipleship for many. To follow Jesus, to be a Spirit-led person, to find and do God's will means to receive new information daily from God regarding all manner of decisions one inevitably confronts.

As a Southern Baptist, I rarely encounter a sermon or participate in a Bible study or small-group session without hearing claims of divine leading and guidance. These claims are shared as though the experience of such daily guidance is a matter of course for speaker and hearer alike. Assumptions and expectations undergirding the normalizing of immediate divine guidance have achieved something like Holy Grail status in many evangelical circles. To challenge the biblical saliency of a daily seeking and receiving of direct divine guidance draws suspicion from the "spiritual ones" who claim this special intimacy with God. Decisions ranging from whom to marry or whether to change jobs to the dilemma of whether to turn left or right on Elm Street all stand open for direct divine input.

Abandonment of such daily seeking and receiving of guidance would seemingly snatch away much of the Christian experience in one fell swoop for many. What remains for the believer besides dead letter legalism once the cherished alertness to the Spirit's leading is lost? Did not Jesus promise that the coming Comforter would teach us all things? It is interesting to note that many followers of Christ now viewed as having obeyed God's will did not claim such immediate divine guidance. Some even rejected such notions as unbiblical and dangerous. Dietrich Bonhoeffer was such a Christian.

Why the almost fierce insistence upon the prudence of daily seeking and finding of divine guidance? Certainly part of the explanation lies in the widespread experience of divine guidance. Many of us who name the name of Jesus Christ testify to profound and, at least to us, undeniable experiences of divine guidance. Claims to such experiences include phenomena ranging from faint nudges to powerful impressions to even verbal instruction.

Let me go on record as claiming certain experiences of divine guidance in my own life. For example, my abandonment of a potential career in engineering for the Christian ministry included almost exactly the three standard expectations of my Southern Baptist tradition in South Carolina: indications of a divine call to ministry; resistance to the call; surrender to the call. Without elaborating, I must confess that I cannot understand my abandonment of engineering for the Christian ministry other than as obedience to the ultimately irresistible call of God. Was this not divine guidance?

It will be helpful to compare Bonhoeffer's understanding of the Christian life with the practice of many evangelicals in our day, especially concerning how one understands knowing and doing the will of God. I do not believe that every dimension of current evangelical pursuit of the Spirit-filled and Spirit-led life deserves censure or falls under a Bonhoeffer-shaped critique. Thus, I want to identify the particular aspects of contemporary practice I have in mind and take an if-the-shoe-fits approach to the relevance and application of critique I expect to emerge.

The illuminist notions I have in view believe that God wants to give fresh and specific guidance for a broad range of daily decisions confronting believers. Concrete guidance covering matters large and small is not only possible but should be expected by Spirit-led believers. Throughout the day one should be open to divine guidance, which could come at any moment, resulting in a left turn rather than a right turn on Pine Street.

Bonhoeffer's understanding of the Spirit-led life and the will of God would seem to contrast sharply with current popular evangelical practice. The focus for Bonhoeffer falls squarely upon obedience to the word of God found in the Bible. As he stated, everything else had become so uncertain. God is not playing hide and seek with his will; he has reveled it to us in Holy Scripture.

Pleasing God

Generally speaking, I expect that the immediacy view will attract many of the most serious and sincere believers among us and with good reason. I find myself in sympathy with those who question the current appetite for daily divine guidance of a more or less direct and nonmoral nature. I also find myself somewhat hesitant and torn as I press a critique against my brothers and sisters on the other side. Part of the explanation for such reticence is my realization that most believers who embrace the ideas in question include many of the best among us. I believe they are sincere. I am convinced of the purity of their motives. They believe God is wise and powerful. They are sure God loves them and has a plan for their lives. So do I. And this final conviction is crucial: they are convinced that God is pleased to give, and wants them to seek, daily guidance on many matters.

Given such convictions, any sincere lover of God will behave just as many now do. They will hold themselves poised for the reception of concrete guidance for the resolution of a wide, often widening, range of daily decisions. They will find themselves predisposed to interpret a wide range of experiences—including especially coincidences, what they call "having a peace," so-called open and closed doors, and internal nudges—as indicators of God's specific will for their lives. And they will, sooner or later, reach conclusions about the accuracy of their discernment in particular cases of supposed guidance. They will find themselves at home with others who live the Christian life in similar openness to ongoing daily divine guidance and will be comfortable hearing accounts of such experiences from them.

Bonhoeffer's alternative view need not shy away from straightforward, unashamed pursuit of "success" in its own way. The difference is that now success must be defined in ways more genuinely biblical. Questions such as: Did we try to help others? Did we actually help others? Did we obey the commands of Scripture, come what may? Did we bear witness to Jesus Christ? now belong to our assessment of the course taken rather than such questions as: Did things work out for me? Were people generally pleased with our actions?

Saying What We Mean

Are we using the language of immediate, specific guidance when what we mean and what we have actually experienced belong to what might be more accurately described as biblical, Spirit-produced illumination and application—the opening of our eyes to the will of God as taught in Scripture in this or that situation calling for action or decision? Bonhoeffer's understanding would seem to welcome such Spirit illuminism.

Yesterday a young man who recently joined the church I pastor approached me at a dinner after Sunday morning services. He casually shared with me that God had told him the night before that he should cease tithing until God either moved him to another congregation or confirmed his membership among us. Now this may be an extreme case and thus a bit of a straw man, easily blown over. But I think this fellow fairly exhibits the Pandora's box of dangers at work in the thinking of many evangelicals today. Note the ease with which the young man could put patently nonbiblical guidance into God's mouth. Furthermore, this brother had not the slightest inkling that any pastor might question the authenticity of his chat with the Master. No, the evangelical landscape he and we inhabit seems to welcome both such easy claims to divine guidance and the ignorance of Scripture exhibited here.

Loss of Comfort of Providence

Surely the comfort of divine providence must rank as one of the most precious treasures of the Christian life. God's providential ruling over the universe and our own lives ensures that the divine purposes in creation and redemption will be fulfilled—this in spite of human weakness and ignorance. Believers across the centuries have borne extraordinary burdens and have even risked their lives for the sake of the gospel undergirded by the promise that God will fulfill his purpose for their lives. Our God can and does hit straight with crooked sticks. Bonhoeffer's resolve and courage included clear convictions concerning divine providence.

Though often unnoticed, the doctrine of providence envisions both a knowing and a not-knowing by God's people. As God's dependent children, we may know all that God chooses to disclose to us of his character and activity and plans for future activity. And indeed, much is disclosed. He has created us; we have sinned. He has provided for our forgiveness, reconciliation, and redemption in Jesus Christ. He abides with us and empowers us for his purposes as God the Holy Spirit. We have a home beyond this world in that city whose builder and maker is God, where there shall be no more pain or crying or death. We shall look into the face of our Savior and be like him. Wow! That is a lot to know! How different our predicament in this world would be if we could not know these things. But we do!

Furthermore, we are given to know that even the evil intentions of men can never ultimately thwart God's good purposes for this world, for his church, and for our own lives. We may not yet see all things under his feet, but that is their destiny, and nothing happens without his will. Yes, Joseph's brothers meant to harm, but God was at work for good, and the good was done. Human and spiritual evil conspired to destroy the spotless Lamb of God on Calvary's cross, but God was actually saving sinners there. Remember Jesus' words to Pilate: "You would have no power over me unless it were given by my Heavenly Father," and, "No one takes my life from me. I lay it down of my own accord."

The doctrine of providence gathers up and celebrates the rich biblical insistence that things are not now and never have been spinning out of control. He's got the whole world in his hands, and he wants us to know this. He also wants us to know that the guarantee that his good purposes will be fulfilled is his own sovereign, powerful, unchanging will to see it done, not our ability to somehow read his cards and thus play the right hand.

Here we begin to recognize the happy ignorance of the children of God. Would we please our Lord? Would we enjoy all the benefits procured by the Savior for those who love him? If so, then we need to know what God has revealed to us and not what he kept to himself. Joseph bears no blame for his ignorance of God's hand in the mistreatment by his brothers while it was happening.

Could it be that some guidance-fixated attempts to know and do God's will unwittingly forfeit much of the comfort of divine providence? By assuming God's desire to "show us his cards" so to speak, we take on a daily burden to seek and receive new, clear, and specific guidance without which we are supposedly "missing God's best." The fulfillment of God's purposes, not only for us but generally, seems to turn upon the waxing and waning of our listening antennas. Little seems left to God to "see to" in his sovereignty and providential ordering of our lives and of history. Gone is the happy sphere of "not needing to know" reserved to God the Father but spared his dependent children. Gone is the cleft of the rock, gone the refuge in God, who knows all and guarantees the fulfillment of his great and glorious plans to deliver and care for his children.

Paralyses

What about those who face future-shaping decisions but cannot claim reception of divine guidance? They must answer, "No, God has not shown me which university to attend, and the deadlines for my response expire in two weeks." "No, I cannot claim leading by the Spirit concerning two job offers awaiting action on my desk."

Many would counsel waiting and praying in such cases as the most prudent course. Otherwise the danger of proceeding either against God's will or at least away from his best plan looms over the guidance-devoid decision. But what if God does not usually offer new, extra-biblical guidance in cases involving nonmoral decision making. And what if, in extraordinary cases in which such guidance is given, God speaks with a biblical clarity corresponding with, say, "Take your sandals off your feet, for the place where you are standing is Holy Ground" (Exod. 3:5). The God of the Old and New Testaments seems to have had little trouble making his will clear when he chose to do so. Yet the will of God for so many today who are caught up in the quest for ongoing guidance seems comparatively murky and elusive, does it not?—almost as though God were playing hide-and-seek with his own children on matters of paramount importance to both them and him.

The result for so many is a kind of paralysis. While surrounded by frequent claims of guidance and divine leadership by others, these "dull" brothers and sisters are left to "pray harder" and wait. But what if God requires no waiting from them? What if God is pleased to have them make decisions, not disregarding the character and will of God revealed in Holy Scripture (God forbid!), but also without needing to claim God's specific and extra-biblical sanction where he has not required it. Is not the burden of decision making in this life heavy enough without taking on more hurdles to jump than God's good plan intended in this respect?

Bonhoeffer found help from Martin Luther to break free from the paralyses that can plague the one who thinks he must justify himself by justifying his decisions and acts as divinely sanctioned. He welcomed Luther's cryptic and controversial mandate for believers to "sin boldly and let grace abound," and to "sin boldly, but believe and rejoice in Christ more boldly still."

Bonhoeffer understood the impossibility of achieving, much less claiming, sinlessness for any human decision or act, and yet we are called to decide and act, and so we must. Not claiming divine sanction for our decisions and actions but, in humility as sinners saved by grace, living by forgiveness and looking to him for justification for the sake of Jesus and his cross, not to our having supposedly latched on to the secrets of God's sovereign movement among us.

Neglect of the Bible

Never have so many had such access to the Bible. Bible production clips along at all-time highs with boutique translations and niche study editions targeting one interest group after another. And, if the pollsters are right, these Bibles are being read by large numbers of people, evangelical believers and otherwise.

But somehow this broad and sustained exposure to the Bible has failed to have the impact one might have expected or hoped for. When divorce rates among evangelicals outpace those within the population at large, our confidence that the Bible is central to the evangelical ethos must wane. When large percentages of our fellow believers doubt the existence of the devil, deny the necessity of sharing their faith, and doubt the sinlessness of Jesus, we have to question how carefully the Bible is being read or whether it is viewed as authoritative for faith and practice within our churches.

Certainly, where a guidance-heavy notion of the Christian life takes hold, the neglect of the Bible should not surprise us. If God stands poised to offer new, daily, extra-biblical instruction, reason and stewardship of time must draw us away from the old word of the Bible to these new, ostensibly more relevant words of God. In such circumstances, inattention to God's new words smacks of neglect, bad stewardship, and ingratitude. And many evangelicals behave precisely according to such reasoning, using the Bible more as prompter to a seeking of something more, or as a confirmer of convictions they bring with them to the text while applying the bulk of their spiritual effort to the quest for some new word from God. Not surprisingly, the Bible is neglected in favor of the pursuit of daily guidance and for literature devoted in whole or in part to that pursuit.

Scripture and Experience

One of the unexamined dimensions of immediacy-dependent approaches to the will of God is the function of human experience. Too often experience is set beside the Bible as a similar source of knowledge, as though one might look first to Scripture and then to experience regarding some particular question and compare the two. Such reasoning seems to require that experience contain meaning of itself, as though the meaning could be, as it were, read off the experience as such. However, such is not the case. Meaning must be given to experience through interpretation, whether conscious or unconscious, according to subjective and epistemologically nonverifiable means.

Bonhoeffer's Reformation-shaped view of sin and its noetic effects, together with his confidence in the authority, sufficiency, and clarity of the Bible, prevented a slide into the murky waters of experience-based Christianity. Bonhoeffer's ability to avoid such pitfalls so associated with Protestant liberalism and later existentialism can be seen in an early marginal note in Reinhold Seeberg's *History of Dogmatics.* In Seeberg we find this: "Luther uses religious experience as well as the Scriptures as the witness and canon of truth. But in this it is experience that establishes the certainty of the truth of the contents of Scripture." This statement provokes particular interest not least because it is made by a Protestant scholar. Bonhoeffer's marginal note reads: "No. On the contrary, it is Scripture that shows the existence of God, and that by way of the Church, the ministry."[47]

The point is not to disparage experience as such or to pit experience against Scripture but rather to recognize the distinction between the two in the field of epistemology. Experience is the place where meaning and truth may be existentially appropriated or, if you will, enjoyed. And thank God for it! We need not resign ourselves merely to being told in Scripture that our sins are forgiven. We may, according to God's good pleasure, experience that this is true and so rejoice from the heart in his mercy. Scripture on the other hand remains as a prompter, shaper, and judge of the meaning of experience.

Sufficiency and Clarity of Scripture

Certainly we can agree that if God expects his children to seek and receive daily guidance on matters ranging from what to wear to whom to marry, then we should, no doubt, get with the program. But what if God has not taught us to seek and expect such things? What if fresh, nonmoral guidance is rare, divinely initiated, and unambiguous? What if God expects believers to make decisions based on what has been called "sanctified reason"—normal human reason only informed by Scripture and so alert to God's character and the great purposes of God revealed there, namely, the advance of the gospel and the edification of the church? What if Bonhoeffer is correct that "we are dependent for knowledge of God upon God's self-revelation alone, testified through the Holy Scriptures and proclaimed through the preaching of the church"?

If these things are so, then the quest for new guidance must come under serious scrutiny. Might the time and effort spent seeking and expecting new information from God be better expended in meditation upon old promises and received blessings? Agonizing over God's specific will for my life might be better channeled into actual obedience to the clear commands of God directed to all of his children in his Word, the Bible!

And if so, it would seem that our plates would be pretty full. Think of the time and energy demanded of us in the advance of the gospel at home and abroad. What of the edification of the church, the making of disciples, the loving of one's enemy? Think of the fruit of the Spirit and the time and effort demanded for its exhibition: love, joy, peace, long-suffering, kindness, goodness, faithfulness, gentleness, self-control (Gal. 5:22, 23). Are guidance-fixated believers comparatively less interested in such things? If so, why? Could it be that they have been encouraged by preaching and popular Christian literature to approach the Christian life more as a strategy for personal happiness than as Bonhoeffer insisted—"when Christ calls a man, he bids him come and die"?[48]

I believe Dietrich Bonhoeffer actually approached the seeking and doing of God's will in such a straightforward way. Such an approach does not always render the finding and doing of God's will simple by any means, but it did provide protection from some of the worst dangers of more subjective, experience-dependent methods.

In his *Cost of Discipleship* Bonhoeffer denies the necessity for some personal revelation in order for believers to know and do the will of God. Bonhoeffer refutes the notion that the first disciples had an advantage over contemporary believers in the discernment of God's will merely by virtue of Jesus' bodily presence. Later within the same chapter he insists that "all we have to do is to hear the word and obey the will of Christ, in whatever part of the Scripture testimony it is proclaimed."[49]

Bonhoeffer addressed the complaint that we Christians, separated from Jesus' earthly existence, stand in a disadvantaged position compared to those privileged to hear his concrete commands firsthand. In the following quote we can see something of Bonhoeffer's conception of simple obedience and also his acknowledgement that the Holy Spirit continues to play a role, not in the dispensing of new revelation but in the reiteration of the one word of God in Holy Scripture:

> The object of Jesus' command is always the same—to evoke wholehearted faith, to make us love God and our neighbor with all our heart and soul. This is the only unequivocal feature of his command. Every time we try to perform the commandment of Jesus in some other sense, it is another sign that we have misunderstood his word and are disobeying it. But this does not mean that we have no means whatever of ascertaining what he would have us do in any concrete situation. On the contrary, we are told quite clearly what we have to do every time we hear the word of Christ proclaimed: yet in such a way that we understand that there is no other way of fulfilling it, but by faith in Jesus Christ alone. Thus the gift Jesus gave to his disciples is just as available for us as it was for them. In fact it is even more readily available for us now that he has left the world, because we know that he is glorified, and because the Holy Spirit is with us.[50]

Two passages prized by defenders of new guidance-fixated discipleship are John 14:26 and 16:13a: "The Helper, the Holy Spirit—the Father will send Him in My name—will teach you all things and remind you of everything I have told you." "When the Spirit of truth comes, He will guide you into all the truth."

Conspicuously, Bonhoeffer, despite his consuming interest in knowing and doing the will of God, made only limited use of these passages. Roman Catholics and Charismatics in particular have cited these passages in support of an ongoing verbal-guidance ministry of the Holy Spirit. Roman Catholics find in them support for the identification of Roman tradition of dogma as revelation. Charismatics point to these passages to defend the normalization of ongoing verbal guidance by the Holy Spirit. And yet leading exegetes from both traditions recognize the unlikelihood of such a reading of these texts. Leading Roman Catholic exegete, Raymond Brown, commenting on John 14:26, contends that "the Paraclete [or Helper] will enable the disciples to see the full meaning of Jesus' words." And, commenting on 16:12–13, Brown warns:

> Does this [verse 13] imply that there will be new revelation after [Jesus' death]? . . . We should be made cautious by comparing [verse 13] to 15:15 which seems to exclude further revelations: "I revealed to you everything I heard from the Father." More likely vs. 12 means that only after Jesus' resurrection will there be full understanding of what happened and was said during the ministry, a theme that is familiar in John. (2:22; 12:16; 13:7)[51]

Brown thus understands "the Helper" in verse 13 as "the one who guides the disciples to the full truth of what Jesus has said."[52]

Simple Obedience

Certainly we can all agree that once God's will is known, the issue of discernment recedes, and the question of obedience or disobedience takes center stage. Discipleship happens as we respond to the call of grace out of spiritual death and into the new life of obedience. In his rejection of cheap grace, Bonhoeffer insists not only that one cannot obey the command of Jesus unless one believes but also that one cannot believe unless one obeys. Protestants are accustomed to the former sequencing but not the latter. Bonhoeffer, like a good Protestant, agrees that faith justifies, not obedience, but he also warns that any chronological sequencing or temporal separation between faith and obedience obscures the actual character of faith as a response to the concrete call and command of Jesus Christ. Thus, faith and obedience are coincident. Faith without works is dead and so is not saving faith at all.

We should note Bonhoeffer's view of the event in which one is confronted with and so encounters the Word of God, whether at conversion or subsequently. This event is characterized by clarity, not ambiguity, simplicity, or complexity. Both the one who calls and the one called realize the transparency of the situation. It is akin to Jesus' call for Peter to leave the boat and make his way to the Lord across the water—quite different from the fogginess and uncertainty surrounding so much discussion of discernment among evangelicals in our day.

Once the expectation that obedience to God's commands will likely lead to suffering of one sort or another has been faced, is not much of the gobbledygook that passes for "steps to the discernment of God's will" exposed as unchristian and irrelevant. Lurking beneath and behind so much that passes for the pursuit of God's will appears to be the pursuit of "success" under the guise of words like "effectiveness" or "finding God's best." Loving one's enemy might not always be a simple matter, but most of us know when we are attempting to do it.

Speaking the Word and Will of God

For Bonhoeffer, the word and will of God are found not only within the pages of Holy Scripture but on the lips of believers—speaking, preaching, admonishing one another. "Where Christians live together the time must inevitably come when, in some crisis, one person will have to declare God's word and will to another."[53] Bonhoeffer does not imagine a second source of revelation alongside the Bible emerging out of the hearts and minds of Christian believers. Bonhoeffer was a convinced Protestant on this issue. No source of revelation exists alongside Holy Scripture. The Bible is not one of many sources of divine revelation but the test of revelational faithfulness for all acts and speech outside itself.

So, no, we do not find in Bonhoeffer any hint of Catholic two-source theory but rather the expectation that the word and will of God revealed in Holy Scripture would find expression within the community of faith. We will explore this issue in more detail in the chapter on community. For now it is enough to recognize that Bonhoeffer envisioned a double responsibility and privilege for believers in relation to the word and will of God.

First of all, each of us enjoys the privilege of hearing the word and will of God from our brothers and sisters in Christ. We may and should expect to hear the voice of God from them, particularly in preaching but in other contexts as well. As we do so, our own faith is challenged and confirmed, and the bond between us and our brother is also confirmed and deepened. None of the benefits of this privilege apply where the mere opinions of my brother or sister are concerned. Only as I hear the actual word and will of God from them are the genuine benefits actualized.

Second, I may and should stand poised to speak the word and will of God to my brother or sister in Christ. As we have already seen, Bonhoeffer recognized the many dangers posed by illuminist and immediacy type claims to speak the word and will of God. Bonhoeffer rejected the identification of one's own thinking or the interpretation of one's experience with the voice of God. But such dangers cannot eliminate the genuine, divinely given privilege and responsibility of speaking the word and will of God within the body of Christ. It has pleased God to bind us to himself and to one another in this way.

chapter Three

THE COMMUNITY
OF BELIEVERS

*"How good and pleasant it is when
brothers can live together!"*

PSALM 133:1

Community

BONHOEFFER'S INTEREST IN THE DOCTRINE of the church
surfaced early during his student days. Already in 1925, as he began
his study with Reinhold Seeberg in Berlin, Bonhoeffer began to
forge the concept of "Christ existing as community."[54] Astonishingly,
Bonhoeffer began his doctoral thesis entitled *Communion Sanctorum*
(The Communion of the Saints) at the age of nineteen. Bonhoeffer

criticized Karl Barth for taking revelation, rather than the church, as his point of departure in his magisterial *Church Dogmatics.* Eberhard Bethge aptly grasped Bonhoeffer's early fixation on the church: "It was to him riddle and aspiration."[55]

Like Friedrich Schleiermacher, the father of Protestant liberalism—and arguably of modern theology as well—Bonhoeffer seems to have been convinced very early that God, and later, Christ, is especially known within the church because he is especially present there. He gives himself to be known within the community of believers and not apart from it. Unlike Schleiermacher, Bonhoeffer did not imagine that knowledge of God could be separated from the knowledge of Christ or that knowledge of Christ could be separated from the testimony of Holy Scripture.

Upon encountering the conception of "Christ existing as community," some critics suspected that Bonhoeffer actually identified Christ with the believing community. Such charges are unfounded. The point was neither to reduce Christ's or God's presence to its manifestation among Christians in fellowship nor to confine divine activity within the church. Rather, Bonhoeffer called for acknowledgment of the church as the sphere in which God is pleased to meet his children. Here God in Christ is pleased to reveal himself and bless and use his children to advance his own purposes in the world. Where individual autonomy and self-fulfillment dominate the Christian self-consciousness and aspiration, access to God is short-circuited. Every believer is set within the body of Christ, the church. No path to Christ exists apart from these actual interdependent relationships between brothers and sisters in Christ within which we now find ourselves set.

Bonhoeffer's early conviction that the nature of the Christian life is essentially communal all but ensured the practical shape his

theology would take. Bonhoeffer excelled within the highly intellectual atmosphere of European university life with its inclination
toward speculation and abstraction, and indeed, he benefited from
the rigors of such discipline. However, Bonhoeffer's pursuit of truth
drove him into the actual world, the concrete world of joy and
suffering where people do not live in isolation but in relationship
and under the pressure of decision making and faced with actual
and pressing problems. In a world where Christians—whether
denominational leaders, pastors, missionaries, or ordinary believers—ask the question, "What works?" the relevance of Bonhoeffer's
writings endures. And yet Bonhoeffer, for all his commitment to
the search for practical solutions to actual problems, would come
to reject felt-relevance as the clue to Christian living. Bonhoeffer
would press questions upon the Bible and expect to find answers
there. What he found was a God determined to have a people, not a
person, for himself. This God came to earth in Jesus Christ not to
make Christians only but a church especially. Still within this communal framework for understanding Christian reality, the individual
remained important and unique.

The Individual

Notwithstanding Bonhoeffer's early and sustained comprehension of the communal character of Christianity, the significance of
the individual was not lost. Bonhoeffer devoted a chapter in *The Cost
of Discipleship* to the individual. He headed that chapter with this passage from Luke's Gospel: "If anyone comes to Me and does not hate
his own father and mother, wife and children, brothers and sisters—
yes, and even his own life—he cannot be my disciple" (Luke 14:26).
Immediately we see that separation from others impinges upon those

called to follow Jesus. Bonhoeffer could even insist that "through the call of Jesus men become individuals."[56]

If perhaps we suffer already from a sense of isolation from others, the call of Jesus threatens to exacerbate that alienation, throwing it into bold relief. I am what I am in God's sight and through Jesus' call with its total claim upon my life. Because of Jesus' call, I discover my true uniqueness and isolation from others. Moreover, Jesus' call demands my decision to acknowledge my separateness, my isolation from those closest to me, putting at risk every relationship but one, namely, to my Lord who calls me.

The call of Jesus compels the displacement of "the things of this world" from the center of my life, taking particular aim at human relationships.[57] Christ must be the center. The world, my natural life, my responsibilities, my relationships, my future, are not annihilated but rather established by the call of Jesus. Their true meaning and potential value are revealed only by the call of Jesus. I may have them back, but only through Jesus Christ. "*He is the mediator*, not only between God and man, but between man and man, between man and reality."[58] Reality is God's view of things. God's last word for humanity is Jesus Christ. Every person is what he or she is in relation to Jesus Christ—nothing more and nothing less.

Bonhoeffer exhibited profound respect for the value of the other person—his worthiness, his uniqueness, his mystery. Friends and acquaintances alike commented on what an intense listener Bonhoeffer was. The distinctive individuality of each person fascinated Bonhoeffer. The collapsing or merging of individual personhood into the divine or the group, though that group be the church, held no attraction for Bonhoeffer. God, according to his good purpose, created individuals, and individuals each must remain. I am who I am, and you are who you are by divine design. The uniqueness of individuality is immutable. Resistance to it fails.

Bonhoeffer's fascination with individuality fueled both his keen interest in other people and his quest for relationship and community. He stooped when speaking with children to achieve eye contact. Children in turn were drawn to him, realizing instinctively that this adult somehow took them seriously. Most importantly, Bonhoeffer recognized that the path to true communion with Christ ran through relationships with others. God had seen to this in creation and in his divine purposes, described most explicitly, perhaps, in 1 Corinthians 12, where the apostle Paul uses the image of the parts of a human body with Christ as head of the body. Bonhoeffer took the interdependence of those parts with utter seriousness, but he also recognized and celebrated the distinctiveness of each part.

Imago Dei

Interest in the church appears early in Bonhoeffer's intellectual pilgrimage and held his attention throughout his life. One suspects that his family's largely formal, almost tangential relationship to the church, combined with his own fellowship-loving personality, contributed to Bonhoeffer's sustained quest for true Christian communion. From as early as his 1924 trip to Rome at age eighteen, the church as a phenomenon had impressed Bonhoeffer. Increasingly, Bonhoeffer became convinced that the meaning of humanity's creation in the image of God (*imago Dei*) included an indispensable relational dimension.

Christ's call to discipleship sets the believer at once into relationship with other believers. Vital membership within the church, the body of Christ, with its privileges and responsibilities, belongs to the essential character of discipleship. None of this should surprise us when we consider that God created us for relationship from the beginning. The Genesis creation account shaped and confirmed Bonhoeffer's early conviction that humanity's dependence on God and others is grounded in the original divine purpose from creation.

Bonhoeffer recognized the inherent relational nature of man in the Genesis account of humanity's creation "in the image of God," or *imago Dei*. The biblical account of humanity's creation *imago Dei* has fascinated believers through the centuries. One dominant approach to the question of the meaning of the creation of human beings in the image of God has been to ask the question, "How are human beings different from the rest of the created order?" Surely in answering this question, so this reasoning argued, we shall discover the meaning of our creation *imago Dei*.

Such investigation has typically produced longer or shorter lists of so-called distinctive human attributes or capacities. Unlike the monkey or the snail darter, so such reasoning goes, man has a moral nature, individual consciousness, perpetuity of existence, the power of contrary choice (true free agency), and anticipation of death and so on. And yet certain biblical passages in question make no such claims in connection with the *imago Dei*. Instead, as Bonhoeffer noted and Barth pursued systematically, what we are told is: "Then God said, 'Let Us make man in Our own image, according to Our likeness. They will rule the fish of the sea, the birds of the sky, the animals, all the earth, and the creatures that crawl on the earth.' So God created man in His own image; He created him in the image of God; he created him; male and female he created them" (Gen. 1:26–27).

The use of the plural, "Let *us* make man," has long intrigued and sometimes baffled biblical expositors of this passage, both Jew and Christian alike. When we consider that acknowledgment of one

God, and one God only, distinguishes true religion from paganism, it is no wonder that Genesis 1:26 has furrowed so many brows across the centuries. Almost all classical exegetes have insisted that this use of the plural anticipates and corroborates the revelation of God as three in one, God the Triune one, especially when viewed alongside other, more explicitly Trinitarian passages.

What has been less often recognized is the connection between the plural "let us" and the answer to the question, what is the *imago Dei* given in the text, namely, "Male and female he created them." As far as Bonhoeffer could see, nothing in the text prompts a search for differences between human beings and snail darters except for humanity's rightful dominion as steward over them, however obvious and appropriate such contrasts might be. Instead, using the language of the grammarian, *imago Dei* and "male and female" stand in apposition. The latter defines or further explains the former. "God created man in his own image; in the image of God he created him; male and female he created them." In what way are human beings created in the image of God? In that they are created male and female!

Here Bonhoeffer is pioneering ground that would be explored further by Karl Barth and others, the *imago Dei* understood not as some quality possessed by the individual. Rather, the creation of humanity *imago Dei* points to humanity's intrinsically relational, communal, mutually interdependent being vis-à-vis other human beings and God. As such, humanity reflects the intratrinitarian communion between the divine Father, Son, and Spirit—thus, the divine plural in Genesis 1:26–27. Barth acknowledged his own dependence on the younger Bonhoeffer and appreciated especially Bonhoeffer's avoidance of the notion of some abstract freedom of humanity. Instead, what we find is a freedom *for* rather than a freedom *from* in humanity's creation. Humanity is free for fellow humanity and for

God as God, is also free according to God's own good pleasure and creative purpose for humanity.

Some extended excerpts from his little booklet *Creation and Fall* should help us understand Bonhoeffer's thinking at this point:

In man God creates his image on earth. This means that man is like the Creator in that he is free. Actually he is free only by God's creation, by means of the Word of God; he is free for the worship of the Creator. In the language of the Bible, freedom is not something man has for himself but something he has for others. No man is free "as such," that is, in a vacuum, in the way that he may be musical, intelligent or blind as such. Freedom is not a quality of man, nor is it an ability, a capacity, a kind of being that somehow flares up in him. . . . Freedom is not a quality which can be revealed—it is not a possession, a presence, an object, nor is it a form of existence—but a relationship and nothing else . . . . Being free means "being free for the other." Because the other has bound me to him. . . . Man differs from the other creatures in that God himself is in him, in that he is God's image in which the free creator views himself. The old dogmatists meant this when they spoke of the inherence of the Trinity in Adam. . . . Man is free by the fact that creature is related to creature. Man is free for man, *Male and female he created them.* Man is not alone, he is in duality and it is in this duality and it is in this dependence on the other that his creatureliness consists. . . . The "image . . . after our likeness" is consequently not an *analogia entis* [analogy of being] in which man, in his being *per se* (through himself) and *a se* (from himself), is in the likeness of the being of God . . . but [an] *analogia relationis* [analogy of relation].[59]

Published in 1937, this piece reveals something of the impressive exegetical head of steam Bonhoeffer had worked up since the completion of this dissertation, *Communio Sanctorum* ("The Communion of Saints") a decade earlier. Bonhoeffer became increasingly convinced of the central place humanity's relational nature played in God's purposes revealed in Jesus Christ.

By creating humanity as male and female, God set man into an inexorable and mutually reinforcing freedom and limit. Arguably the two most primordially intuitable dimensions of the self-consciousness are, first, that *we*, like the opposite sex but unlike other living creatures, are human. Second, I am either male or female. Unity in distinction! By myself I cannot represent humanity fully any more than my opposite-sex counterpart can. Humanity is not male or female or any mixture of the two but the two together in relationship marked by mutual interdependence. Both sexes are essential to the survival of the human race. Despite his pleasure in the created order prior to the creation of humanity, God failed to see himself reflected there. Human beings—uniquely and exclusively—would be capable of reflecting the Creator as in a mirror.

The Gift of Community

Bonhoeffer embraced the great promises of God to his people. He anticipated blessings from the hand of the heavenly Father, but he understood that the largest part of these blessings comes only at the Last Day, at the inauguration of the coming universal reign of Christ. Even the full enjoyment of Christian fellowship must await the second coming of Christ and entrance into the next world where crying and pain and death and loneliness, too, are no more. Accordingly, John the apostle anticipates worship and fellowship together with the saints of all ages in the vision of the Revelation. The demands of following Christ themselves often prevent direct enjoyment of personal fellowship between believers. Paul's obedience to the missionary mandate took him away from cherished brothers and sisters. Obedience to Jesus' command to preach landed Paul in prison more than once, where he longed to "see the face" of Timothy once more.

"The believer feels no shame . . . when he yearns for the physical presence of other Christians. . . . The prisoner, the sick person, the Christian in exile sees in the companionship of a fellow Christian a physical sign of the gracious presence of the triune God" (LF, 19–20).[60]

And so while Bonhoeffer highly valued Christian fellowship, even identifying it as a constituent dimension of true communion with God himself, the pursuit of such fellowship could never provide an excuse for disobedience, an occasion for laying down one's cross. As David Dockery has recognized, "Happiness is the promise of heaven . . . holiness is the priority here in this world."[61] Freedom to worship and serve our Lord in the visible church with our brothers and sisters in Christ is a great blessing, a special mercy. It constitutes a concrete anticipation of and dress rehearsal for the true and permanent fellowship of the saints in the next world.

Bonhoeffer understood that the pursuit of fellowship, like other human urges, is susceptible to narcissistic and hedonistic impulses. Yet, the hunger, indeed the need, for Christian communion has its source in God's good creation and express purpose. It is right for the Christian prisoner or missionary or exiled apostle to yearn for contact with fellow believers. The absence, not the presence, of such longings would call into question one's relationship to Christ. We were made for one another, and our relationship with Christ includes our divinely created and sustained connection to one another. It is a life-giving, mutually interdependent connection as described in 1 Corinthians 12.

For Bonhoeffer, we misunderstand the constituent role of the community for the Christian life if we reduce it to a means for our individual enjoyment of other supposed blessings. Though not simply wrong, it is a distortion to think of the church as mainly the path to the benefits of knowing Christ. This is so particularly in reference to the concrete, local church—Bonhoeffer tended to say "visible community"—to which the believer is attached. Rather, this fellowship belongs to the divinely determined destination of the disciple; it belongs to the benefits themselves. There can be no knowing of Christ in the fullest sense apart from this fellowship. This divinely created and sustained community both forms the context in which the benefits of Christ become accessible to the disciple and constitutes itself one of those benefits.

Finkenwalde

In the face of Hitler's spies and censors, the Confessing Church eventually felt compelled to provide theological education to its ministers "underground," as it were. Bonhoeffer seized this opportunity to experiment with some of his ideas about Christian community. In 1935, during the first term of the new seminary, Hitler established a church ministry composed of committees charged with "pacifying" the church. The ranks of the Confessing Church were greatly reduced over the question of whether to cooperate with the new committees. On December 2, 1935, Reich Minister Hans Kerrl issued a decree "for the Implementation for the Law for the Protection of the Evangelical Churches," which had the effect of outlawing the Preacher's Seminary at Finkenwalde. That evening Bonhoeffer met with the student ordinands, releasing them from their commitment should they choose to leave. They all stayed, and for two years Bonhoeffer conducted something of an experiment in Christian community.

Finkenwalde, a tiny community near Stettin on the Polish side of the German border, provided Bonhoeffer with a much-needed respite from the usual demands he typically endured. The first chapters of his famous book *The Cost of Discipleship* were written there. In October 1937, Hitler's police shut down the seminary. The following year, Bonhoeffer published *Gemeinsames Leben* (published in 1939 in English under the title *Life Together*), describing his experiment at Finkenwalde. Bonhoeffer's leadership at Finkenwalde offers a unique window into his developing vision of the Christian life and the church.

Life Together opens with Bonhoeffer's theological rationale for the structure he imposed upon the students seeking ordination at Finkenwalde. He begins with what might be the most foundational theological conviction of his thought, the centrality of Jesus Christ. It is interesting to note that Karl Barth, the most significant theological influence upon Bonhoeffer, was most proud of the charge that his theology "suffered from christomonism"—the reduction of Christianity to Jesus Christ. Obviously Barth rejected the pejorative intent of such critiques together with the suggestion that his theology involved a reductionistic distortion of the biblical message. Instead, he insisted that only through Jesus Christ can the whole scope of God's revelation be understood aright. Jesus Christ is not only the fulfillment of God's revelation but is God himself, the Word made flesh, dwelling among us, the one concrete divine self-disclosure in space and time. Certainly Bonhoeffer embraced this aspect of Barth's thinking. In fact, Bonhoeffer's infrequent, and often enigmatic, criticisms of Barth tended to suggest that Barth had failed to remain true to his own best insights in the field of Christology.

In any case Bonhoeffer's quest for true Christian community was, first of all, a quest for communion in and with Jesus Christ and, through him, with one another. We only belong to one another through Jesus Christ, but in him we do indeed belong to one another. As members of his body, we need one another, and in him we recognize our election, from all eternity, to know not only God but also ourselves in the community whose head is Jesus Christ (1 Cor. 12).

Because our relationships to one another are created and determined by our relationship to Jesus Christ, they must reflect our status as the redeemed, adopted children of God. The community of believers is made up exclusively of sinners justified by grace through faith in Jesus Christ and him crucified, risen, and ascended to the heavenly Father. The implication of this fact for the true church is constitutive and profound.

For one thing, as a justified sinner, I have no interest in using my brother as a means to my own salvation in the strict sense. It is true that I am inextricably bound to fellow believers upon incorporation into Christ and that all paths to my Savior run through, not around or apart from, the church. Nevertheless, in Jesus Christ, I am confronted with the completed work of atonement and reconciliation for myself and for my brother. We both live not from ourselves but from Christ, our living head. The righteousness by which we both live and on the basis of which we meet one another is not our own. It is that alien righteousness of which Luther spoke—the righteousness of Christ applied to those found in him. Now I am free for my brothers and sisters—free to love and serve them, free also to be loved and served by them in the special freedom enjoyed only by forgiven sinners.

Word and Fellowship

Bonhoeffer developed a distinctive notion of the so-called "worldliness" of Christianity, which we will take up again in the chapter on witness and relevance. One aspect of this "worldliness" view emphasizes not only the responsibility of the church for the world but also the common humanity of all peoples. However, Bonhoeffer did not deem this common humanity a sufficient basis for Christian community. Only the Word of God binds disciples of Jesus together in true Christian fellowship.

Our common humanity binds us to all peoples, but our reception of the word of God separates us from the world and creates Christian community. The believer receives the word of God, especially the word spoken in Jesus Christ, and even more especially, the word of the cross. The word of the cross exposes, judges, and forgives sin and, significantly, reveals and shapes what we must understand as the Christian life, the life of discipleship. The cross demands that followers of Jesus give their lives for the sake of others, first of all for fellow believers and then also for the world for whom Christ died. Such imitation of Christ never imagines itself as a supplement to the one all-sufficient sacrifice of the one mediator, the spotless Lamb of God for the world. Rather, this imitation stands as a witness to its crucified and risen Savior.

Christ the Center

Individuality is not compromised but realized in fellowship, in community, with others. We belong to one another by design. We were created for relationship with one another, and we do truly belong to one another in and through Jesus Christ. For Bonhoeffer, in Jesus

Christ and in him alone we belong to one another, not in Gandhi, or Buddha, or anyone else, just Jesus Christ and him alone.

We dare not miss this point—Bonhoeffer's exclusive identification of Jesus Christ as the means to true fellowship, true community, and more, true humanity. His interest in Eastern religion generally and Gandhi in particular may tempt some to a pluralistic reading of Bonhoeffer's work. Theological liberals and progressives may chafe at the exclusive claims of Christ belonging to ancient, orthodox, biblical, Christian witness, but Bonhoeffer did not. Not surprisingly, unlike many Protestant liberals, Bonhoeffer did not suffer from a bad conscience regarding the Christian mandate to proselytize.

No doubt, insatiable curiosity drove Bonhoeffer in many directions. He was interesting because he was interested. And Bonhoeffer was ready to receive practical help from any quarter, including other religions. But a fair reading of the Bonhoeffer corpus ensures rejection of pluralistic construals of his interest in Eastern religion. A better explanation lies in the direction of the taking captive of all things under Christ who, for Bonhoeffer, was indeed the Lord of this world. Bonhoeffer's interest in Gandhi is comparable to the current church growth interest in the concepts of leadership and managerial theory. For Bonhoeffer only the call of Jesus Christ makes one a child of God and sets one within the body of Christ.

Jesus calls individuals to himself and to the life of discipleship separately, not in groups. Each must come alone. And entrance into the fellowship of the believing community involves no shedding or compromise of one's individuality but rather the yielding of the whole self to the community for service. And this reality and service, established and nurtured only in Christ and him crucified, will necessarily involve suffering as a constituent dimension of its conformity to Christ (Rom. 8:17). This suffering must come because of the identification of the disciple with his lord. Our obedience to him and witness to him will bring to us the same reception he received—rejection, persecution, and perhaps death.

Community under the Word

Bonhoeffer pursued his vision of a believing community at the underground seminary at Finkenwalde. Having ministered in London, New York, and Spain, Bonhoeffer developed a keen sympathy for the special burdens of isolation and loneliness common to many pastors. Though not a local congregation in the usual sense, the underground seminary at Finkenwalde provided a unique opportunity for Bonhoeffer to test some of his convictions concerning Christian fellowship and address certain needs of pastors. He longed for and sought to construct conditions conducive to the nurturing of true Christian community at Finkenwalde, a community where Christ is at the center.

Perhaps the best characterization of those conditions is the conception of a community "under the word of God." The notion of freedom is prominent in Bonhoeffer's thinking, and yet this image of a community under the Word of God recognizes restriction and prohibition, boundaries and mutual consideration, as necessary to Christian community. Only submission to the Word of God promises true freedom to followers of Jesus Christ. His expectation that students would spend time in meditation on a common, relatively short, selected passage highlighted his desire to have fellowship within the community shaped by the Scriptures.

Not an Ideal but a Divine Reality

Two dimensions of Bonhoeffer's theological rationale for the Finkenwalde experiment deserve special attention because of their practical implications for the church today and are summarized in *Life Together* as follows: "In Christian brotherhood everything depends upon its being clear right from the beginning, first that Christian brotherhood is not an ideal, but a divine reality. Second, that Christian brotherhood is a spiritual and not a [human] reality."[62]

Bonhoeffer believed that many Christian fellowships had been destroyed by what he called the "wish dream" of idealism. Clearly Bonhoeffer held himself, at least from a worldly point of view, to what can only be viewed as spectacularly high standards as a disciple of Jesus Christ. After all, he not only declared that "when Jesus calls a man, he bids him come and die," he consciously and with both relief and also fear and trembling, exposed himself to likely death when he left the safety of New York in June 1939. And he did so against the urgings of many friends, determined, should his life be spared, to do everything in his power to retain credibility in the rebuilding of a new Germany.

Bonhoeffer viewed the congregation as the assembly of forgiven sinners, not only saved by grace but sustained by grace, and who must live by forgiveness and grace. New believers often enter the church under the illusion that others and they themselves will quickly need less and less of forgiveness as they ascend the heights of holy living. But it is not so. Instead, it is precisely within the church that believers are called to reflect in their relationships with others the forgiveness and mercy they themselves have enjoyed in Christ. And they too will require a great measure of forbearance from others within the congregation.

What a recovery of biblical realism Bonhoeffer's insight represents! The concrete naming of the fruit of the Spirit alone should have disabused us of the "wish dream" idealism against which Bonhoeffer warned. Clearly God expects that the usual experience of the believer will provide occasion for patience, forbearance, confession of sin, the restoration of sinners in gentleness, and forgiveness. Occasions calling for the exercise of loving church discipline will be the norm, not the exception.

Of course, the occasion and demand for forgiveness never suggested tolerance for sin whatsoever. Note this passage from *Cost of Discipleship*: "Cheap Grace is the preaching of forgiveness without requiring repentance, baptism without church discipline, communion without confession, absolution without personal confession."[63] So tolerance of sin—no! The presence of sinners (including oneself)—yes! Indeed an integral part of the believing community's purpose as a living reflection of the very grace by which they constituted the people of God is at stake in how sinners are treated within the church.

A Spiritual, Not a Human, Reality

Bonhoeffer recognized that God the Holy Spirit alone puts Jesus Christ into the hearts of believers. And the community of faith is founded solely on Jesus Christ. Thus, Christian fellowship is essentially a spiritual and not a human reality. Where genuine Christian community appears, God creates and sustains it by his Spirit indwelling its members.

Against sanguine and optimistic estimations of human nature so prominent within liberal and progressive theologies, Bonhoeffer took a dim view of humanity in its "natural" state. In the cross of Jesus, the truth of both human depravity and divine grace are displayed:

> The basis of all spiritual reality is the clear, manifest Word
> of God in Jesus Christ. The basis of all human reality is
> the dark, turbid urges of the human mind. The basis of the
> community of the Spirit is truth; the basis of [unredeemed]
> human community is desire. The essence of the commu-
> nity of the Spirit is light, for "God is light, and in him is no
> darkness at all" (1 John 1:5) and "if we walk in the light,
> we have fellowship one with another" (1:7). The essence
> of [natural] human community of spirit is darkness, "for
> from within, out of the heart of men, proceed evil thoughts"
> (Mark 7:21). It is the deep night that hovers over the
> sources of all human action, even over all noble and devout
> impulses.[64]

Only the Holy Spirit of God who became incarnate in Jesus Christ empowers something other than, indeed opposite to, self-seeking, lust-driven, human motivation and action. And, thanks be to God, he does just that. God the Spirit creates and enables a community character-ized by self-sacrificing love.

This life-giving power never becomes the possession of the believ-ing community. God's love-shaped, community-creating power never operates like, say, the energy provided by exercise, amphetamines, or a course on positive thinking. Such, shall we say, nonspiritual, mun-dane empowerment—no doubt genuine and legitimate in its own way—passes into the hands of, comes under the control of, those it aids for use according to their own wills. Not so with empowerment of the Holy Spirit. God's empowerment, the Holy Spirit, is God himself. We never snatch God's power for use in pursuit of our own desires. Attempts to do so are futile and inevitably lead to wrongheaded and unnecessary frustration and disappointment with God as we blame him for not making good on promises never given.

Tragically, we Christians frequently lapse, albeit unwittingly perhaps, into quasi-pagan approaches to God, fashioning a "god" according to our own desires, and subsequently expect the idol to do our bidding. But of course these idols are our own creation. Phantoms that they are, they remain powerless. Bonhoeffer took Barth's critique of what he called "religion" to heart. Where the revelation of God in Jesus Christ is not recognized, where the vertical coming down of god to man in the incarnation is not confronted, the critique of Ludwig von Feuerbach applies. We project into the metaphysical realm our own highest human hopes, dreams, and fantasies and fashion a god we climb up to and then prompt to do our bidding. But these "gods" are nothing but idols and can do nothing.

God's power always and only accomplishes God's purposes. But, alas, God's power assuredly does accomplish his purposes, and those purposes are not hidden but revealed to us in his Word! One of the clearest, most central of those purposes is precisely God's intention to have a people for himself, the church, where forgiven sinners are adopted into the family of God in Jesus Christ. They are incorporated into the body of Christ, built up in love, and deployed as Christ's witnesses to his glory.

The practical consequence of this realization is staggering in its clarity and aim. We may pursue Jesus Christ within his church with the firm confidence that he is pleased we are doing his will, and his empowerment will sustain us. Pursuit of God's revealed will, using revealed means, never proves abortive. Victory is assured.

Confession

Even after his break with Roman Catholicism, Martin Luther, who Bonhoeffer cites more often than any other figure, wished to retain a modified form of confession for the new Protestant churches. However, it was exposure to the many serious faces entering and emerging from the confessionals of St. Peter's in Rome in 1924 that first turned Bonhoeffer's attention to the importance of this ancient practice. In this connection it is interesting to recall the first of Luther's ninety-five theses: "When our Lord and Master Jesus Christ said, 'Repent' [Matt. 4:17], he willed the entire life of believers to be one of repentance."[65] In Luther's explanation of the theses, he rejects the Roman doctrine of sacramental penance administered by the clergy but calls for the practice of confession among believers who act as "priests" to each other. As Luther before him, so Bonhoeffer sought to recover this neglected aspect of the original Protestant doctrine of the priesthood of all believers. Many Protestants and, later, evangelicals, had embraced the vertical implications of that doctrine, namely, individual access to God through Jesus Christ, the one mediator between God and humanity. Far fewer, though, even considered the horizontal dimensions, such as the benefits and responsibilities wherein believers speak the word of God to one another for mutual edification and admonition. Confession of sin belongs to this horizontal dimension, and Bonhoeffer recognized the community-building fruit that mutual confession promised within the body of Christ.

Bonhoeffer retained a Protestant denial of any sacramental "magic" associated with confession or with any other straightforward obedience to biblical teaching. And, while he recognized certain limitations and dangers of confession—as one might with other established Christian activities as long as us sinners are involved, including prayer, preaching or evangelism—the benefits denied in its absence impressed him more. Reflecting on his experience at St. Peter's, he wrote, "Confession does not necessarily lead to scrupulous living:

often, however, that may occur and always with the most serious
people."[66]

Bonhoeffer's attraction to the retention of mutual confession was
of a piece with his desire to see a community shaped by the Word
of God. In his understanding of the proclamation of the Word, he
envisioned not only the witness directed to unbelievers but also the
word proclaimed by brother to brother for mutual edification and
admonition:

> Where Christians live together the time must inevitably
> come when in some crises one person will have to declare
> God's word and will to another. . . . It is inconceivable that
> the things that are of utmost importance to each individual
> should not be spoken by one to another. It is unchristian
> consciously to deprive another of the one decisive service
> we can render to him. If we cannot bring ourselves to utter
> it, we shall have to ask ourselves whether we are not still
> seeing our brother garbed in his human dignity which we
> are afraid to touch, and thus forgetting the most important
> thing, that he, too, no matter how old or highly placed or
> distinguished he may be, is still a man like us, a sinner in
> crying need of God's grace.[67]

Although in no way central to Bonhoeffer's ethics, he did take a
stab or two at developing a method for decision-making. The second
step of a three-part procedure reads, "I should never act alone, firstly
because I need the advice of the brothers, secondly because the brothers need me, and thirdly because there is a church discipline which
I must not treat lightly."[68]

Community in Prison

Following his arrest by the Gestapo on April 5, 1943, Bonhoeffer was consigned to solitary confinement. Because Bonhoeffer was a political prisoner, even the guards were, at first, forbidden to speak with the accused preacher turned conspirator in the attempted assassination of Adolf Hitler. Bonhoeffer, who had instructed aspiring young seminarians in the art of being alone, being silent, and meditating on the Word of God, now found himself plunged into despair at the loss of mundane human fellowship. Bonhoeffer also feared that he might betray friends under interrogation. A scrap of paper preserved from the early weeks of his imprisonment reveal that Bonhoeffer considered the possibility that suicide might be his duty under such circumstances.

In prison Bonhoeffer had confirmed the crucial, divinely created communal nature of humanity and Christian existence when he was allowed to receive visitors. Visits from two pastors in particular refreshed his soul. Pastor Dannenbaum of the Berlin city mission read the Bible to him and led intercessory prayer. Pastor Harold Poelchau also visited Bonhoeffer's cell to offer support, even illegally, putting himself at risk in order to give comfort to those in prison as Jesus had admonished. Bonhoeffer kept up his daily regimen of Bible study, meditation on the Word, and prayer. He found himself grateful to the point of tears that he had memorized so many of Paul Gerhardt's hymns.

In time Bonhoeffer found the sustaining grace of God available to him in prison. God restored his spirit so that he really became the pastor of a little flock there. He led in Bible study and prayer when possible and encouraged his fellow inmates. From the spring of 1943 religious services were forbidden, and Bonhoeffer found himself unaffected in the main. Still, at times his heart would well up with longing for public worship and singing praises to God in unison with others.

While in prison many of Bonhoeffer's earlier insights crystallized and reemerged with new vigor and clarity. From his prison cell Bonhoeffer writes:

> I remember a conversation that I had in America thirteen years ago with a young French pastor. We were asking ourselves quite simply what we wanted to do with our lives. He said he would like to become a saint (and I think it's quite likely that he did become one). At the time I was very impressed, but I disagreed with him, and said, in effect, that I should like to learn to have faith. For a long time I didn't realize the depth of the contrast. I thought I could acquire faith by trying to live a holy life, or something like it. I suppose I wrote *The Cost of Discipleship* as the end of that path. Today I can see dangers of that book, though I still stand by what I wrote.[69]

What were the dangers or, perhaps better, the blind spots Bonhoeffer detected in his classic on discipleship? What was the basis of his disagreement with the French pastor? Between the 1939 publication of *The Cost of Discipleship* and his arrest in April 1943, Bonhoeffer experienced no radical break from his previous views, but his conviction that the Christian life is a matter of service within and from the church to the world intensified. So also did his grasp of certain emphases of the Reformation. From Martin Luther and to some extent also from Karl Barth, Bonhoeffer saw that discipleship meant living out of grace and promise received rather than the quest to achieve something for oneself. In a 1936 letter to a girlfriend, Bonhoeffer identified "ambition" as the unchristian element in his ministry prior to his "discovery of the Bible." The point was not to disparage either sainthood or faith but rather to reject both as ultimate goals and to confess the finished work of Christ on the cross in word and deed, perhaps especially deed. Upon reflection Bonhoeffer winced at the spiritual narcissism that characterized not only the views of the French pastor but the whole tenor of the conversation they shared.

In a day when Christianity is so frequently offered as one more strategy for personal happiness, Bonhoeffer's insight surely falls like a thunderclap upon our ears. Also, in the aforementioned letter, Bonhoeffer confesses his sin and celebrates his liberation to a better way:

> I know that at that time I turned the doctrine of Jesus
> Christ into something of personal advantage for myself. . . .
> I pray to God that that will never happen again. Also I had
> never prayed, or prayed only very little. For all my loneli-
> ness, I was quite pleased with myself. Then the Bible, and
> in particular the Sermon on the Mount, freed me from
> that. Since then everything has changed. I have felt this
> plainly, and so have other people around me. It was a great
> liberation. It became clear to me that the life of a servant of
> Jesus Christ must belong to the Church, and, step by step it
> became plainer to me how far that must go. (DB, 154–55)[70]

Idealism Begone

Christ expected obedience to his commands, pure and simple. The command was concrete, worldly, directed to disciples there and then. Leave your nets. Follow me. Love your enemies. Christ did not set up ideals for adoration but issued directives to be followed straight away. Likewise the fellowship of believers within the Christian com-munity ought to be characterized by certain values, qualities, and practices reflecting the lordship of Jesus among them. Forgive one another. Bear one another's burdens. But also, rebuke, reprove, correct, and even treat him like a pagan!

Bonhoeffer's quest for worldliness is a call for concreteness, for actual living obedience in space and time and especially in reference to the church. Already during his student days, Bonhoeffer's interest centered upon the church, and particularly the actual living congregation of believers as opposed to theoretical and idealistic notions of the church. Not that Bonhoeffer dismissed the importance of developing a theology of the church; he did not, but his impatience along with the momentous events that engulfed Germany with the rise of the Third Reich compelled Bonhoeffer to address the concrete necessities of church life with unusual vigor.

As we have noted, the Christian community, for Bonhoeffer, is not an ideal but a divine reality. It would be difficult to overestimate the centrality of this conviction in Bonhoeffer's understanding of his own vocation as a minister of the Word of God.

Bonhoeffer expects believers, and especially serious Christians, to fall into the exact error he fears: "The serious Christian, set down for the first time in a Christian community, is likely to bring with him a very definite ideal of what Christian life together should be and to try to realize it" (LT, 26).[71] What is wrong with such a hope? Much, according to Bonhoeffer. And most of these dangers center on the attempt to use the community of believers as a vehicle for personal aspiration rather than as the means and context for service to God and others.

Thirst for Community

One explanation for Bonhoeffer's early and enduring fascination with the doctrine of the church is that the subject was, as Bethge has noted, "in the air" during his student days. Luminaries such as Paul Althaus and, notably, Karl Barth published significant works addressing the subject. The youth movement in Germany and Europe generally exhibited keen interest as well. The renaissance of the study of the dismal Dane, Søren Kierkegaard, brought his *Attack on Christendom* into view.

However that may be, evangelicals at the beginning of the twenty-first century are experiencing a renewed interest, if not in the doctrine of the church as such, certainly in the quest for community. With the waning, if not the collapse of denominational loyalty in America, the mobility of evangelicals between congregations has never been greater. Local churches minister in a highly competitive, Christian-consumer, winner-take-all environment. Perhaps as never before, joining a church may do little to satisfy the current self-conscious search for community.

Forbidding Terrain

What if we somehow find within ourselves the thirst for community Bonhoeffer experienced? What if we find inescapable the biblical truism that the path to deep relational intimacy with Jesus runs through relationships with our brothers and sisters in Christ? If, perchance, we commit ourselves to a more biblical, covenant-shaped relationship with our fellow believers, we can expect rough sledding. The terrain is forbidding.

Barriers to the pursuit of genuine Christian community abound. David Wells surveys some of these in his books *No Place for Truth* and *God in the Wasteland.*[72] Secularization, urbanization, and technological innovation have transformed the cultural landscape in ways often hostile to the establishing and nurturing of community of any kind, including Christian community. Secularism encourages or even enforces restriction of religion and spirituality to the private sphere, feeding the individualistic tendencies already rooted in the Western psyche. Secular society may tolerate a bland, intellectually disinterested affirmation of religious diversity and pluralism in the public square, but it prefers to hear nothing of religion at all. A "me and Jesus" spirituality, kept safely hidden in one's closet, seems perfectly suited to pacify secular prickliness with respect to individual piety.

The urbanization of America—and, indeed, of the world—exposes and exacerbates an array of human tendencies and behaviors typically incompatible with sustained fellowship. Residents settle into lives of isolation, anonymity, and freedom from responsibility and accountability that true Christian community would prevent. They also suffer the loss of the special support, encouragement, and haven from the stresses of urban life the church should provide to urban believers. Increasingly the suburbs facilitate similar patterns of anonymity and isolation.

Economic forces encourage mobility and impermanence. Community takes time to build and nurture. Suburban living too provides a hospitable environment for anonymous living in which the compartmentalization of one's relational spheres militates against—or shields one from, depending on one's perspective—the development of genuine communities where mutual responsibility and accountability to others could flourish.

Technological innovation—admitting the dazzling and positive contributions made in the fields of medicine and communication, for example—also render the search for community problematic. The telephone allows convenient and widespread converse but also allows us to stay apart. The Internet, with its e-mail and chat rooms, facilitates a kind of cyberspace relationship which, while no doubt meaningful in its own way, falls far short of the kind of mutually interdependent and covenant-commitment-shaped fellowship envisioned in a biblical community of faith.

Multiple televisions, headphones, and, in the suburbs, the exponential increase in the average square footage of single-family homes hurl family members centrifugally outward within the same dwelling, as each sinks into his own chosen peopleless world. No wonder so many of us, when forced into a social setting, feel disoriented by the strange necessity to relate to actual persons who cannot be surfed past with the click of the mouse.

Increasingly, especially in the urban metroplexes, believers behave and think, and are encouraged to think, of themselves as Christian consumers shopping for Christian products and services. In such an environment Christianity, the gospel, or if you will, Jesus, becomes a product to be marketed. Leaving aside the threat such a market-fashioned landscape poses to the content of the gospel itself—what with its seeker-insensitive turnoffs such as repentance from sin and warnings of eternal punishment—this consumer-oriented landscape allows for a kind of church shopping and church hopping inconducive to true Christian community. The New Testament envisions communities of faith where patience, long-suffering, and forgiveness characterize the normal means by which spiritual gifts are displayed. Today many of us simply drive away from the necessity to put up with anything negative, especially our brothers and sisters in Christ who require patience, long-suffering, and forgiveness.

Plainly Bonhoeffer's vision of true Christian community contrasts sharply with such a Christian consumer-driven atmosphere. The church God builds envisions covenant commitment, mutual interdependence, and a clinging to, standing by, and loving of one another reflective of the love we have known in Jesus Christ.

What to Do?

Clearly the obstacles to rich Christian community are formidable, and, no doubt, some of the conditions particularly suited to foster true fellowship lie outside our power to produce. And we should remember that sometimes obedience to Christ may itself hinder our enjoyment of the kind of fellowship we yearn to experience.

With fellowship, it takes two or more to tango, and others might not cooperate with our determination to have them stay put and facilitate our quest for Christian community. Even if I deliberately settle down with my present congregation, others undoubtedly will leave for one reason or the other. Indeed, I may find some compelling reason to move on as well. Still, once we recognize what is forfeited where the Christian consumer mentality takes over and becomes the norm, there are changes we can make that can render true Christian fellowship more possible.

Stop running! We can resist interpreting difficulties within the church common to human relationships as grounds (by themselves at least) to consider severing those ties. Where long-suffering, patience, kindness, forgiveness, and love must mark true disciples, relational trouble need not trigger a round of church hunting but rather occasion the necessary and expected display and exercise of spiritual authenticity. As Christ has done in regard to us, so ought we do to others. We bear with the wayward and troublesome brother, recognizing that this belongs to discipleship and shapes the context in which each of us matures as a Christian. And we soberly admit that sustained fellowship will demand similar spiritual accommodation and bearing-up by others in relation to ourselves! It is a two-way street. And such bearing-up and forgiving, for Bonhoeffer, will not find the exercise of church discipline contradictory to its aims but rather as necessary and loving.

Once we recognize that the path to Christ and the path to biblical self-fulfillment runs only through the community of faith, we gain solid incentives to settle somewhere and let ourselves sit all the way down in the pew, embracing our inextricable, divinely willed, and thus ultimately redemptive siblinghood with the believers around us. It feels good and right to attempt this because it is both.

Warn and recover others. Despite the truly difficult cultural impediments to the experience of rich and authentic Christian fellowship, many believers are teachable and can successfully change the way they understand the role of the church in their lives, and God will help! Confusion and frustration result when we try to enlist God in the quest to realize our own dreams and fantasies, but the search for true Christian community, with all its attendant responsibilities and benefits, involves obedience to God's own command. For this the power of the Holy Spirit is surely available.

Several families joined a small southern Indiana church I pastored during my postgraduate studies. Given the history of this and many other churches, I feared that these families would likely drift away from the congregation following my departure. After announcing my intention to accept a teaching position in Missouri, I called a meeting with the families and asked them to describe what their church experience would be like in a perfect world. Much of their response could be accurately captured with two words—belonging and significance. They wanted to experience a family-like belonging with their fellow believers, and they wanted to know that their own presence, their own gifts, were needed. They wanted to serve within a true family of faith.

I pointed out that many of the longtime members of the church were already enjoying these things. They recognized that this was so. I went on to argue that one indispensable key to their own enjoyment of such community was simply that they stay put. I encouraged them, at least mentally and emotionally, to burn a bridge, to determine that these folk would be their church family. I pointed out that, in order to reach their own stated goals, they would likely have occasions to forgive and ask for forgiveness, to bear with the weaknesses and failings of others and have their own borne with as well. Before my departure, I preached sermons on the church from 1 Corinthians and Ephesians, developing more fully the biblical vision for life in Christian community. Most of these families stayed and have now achieved much of what they yearned for and thought impossible to gain.

Chapter Four

WITNESS AND RELEVANCE

*Where the question of relevance
becomes the theme of theology, we can
be certain that the cause has already
been betrayed and sold out. . . . The
intention should not be to justify
Christianity in this present age, but
to justify the present age before the
Christian message.*[73]

DIETRICH BONHOEFFER

IN SO MANY WAYS Bonhoeffer's ever-emerging ministerial identity
seems the antithesis of the ivory-tower stereotype. True, he was a

scholar, and he never viewed his research as in competition with his interest in ministry. Indeed, Bonhoeffer yearned for more freedom to spend time with his books. And yet Bonhoeffer experienced an inner compulsion to plunge into the fray of living, confronting the world with all its complexity and difficulty. Bonhoeffer accepted the importance of relevance as one indicator of true discipleship. And yet Bonhoeffer never imagined the church finding its message in the world. The church brings its own message to the world. The disciple bears witness of Jesus Christ to the world. In this chapter we will explore the distinctive relationship between relevance and witness in Bonhoeffer's thinking.

Monasticism

Bonhoeffer's ambivalent assessment of the monastic movement illuminates certain features of his conception of the church as relevant witness within the world. Bonhoeffer never lost his respect for what monastics had gotten exactly right—namely, that following Christ involves a costly enterprise marked by self-denial, sacrifice, and inevitable suffering. But insofar as the monk's retreat from the world becomes permanent and becomes a strategy for the pursuit of the monk's own holiness, it must be rejected as unchristian. The church, which was right to tolerate monasticism and incorporate its protest against the secularization of the church, was wrong to recognize the "fatal double standard" wherein the masses settle for a supposed minimal yet nevertheless still genuine standard of Christian discipleship while a few especially serious believers pursue the supposed higher call replete with vows of poverty, chastity, and obedience. Witness, the duty and privilege of the whole church, not the prerogative of a select few, plunges disciples into the world as they accept responsibility for the world as followers of Christ.

Bonhoeffer's nuanced assessment of the monastic movement drew upon Martin Luther's pilgrimage, first into and then out of the cloistered life. According to Bonhoeffer, both decisions, first to embrace and then to renounce monastic vows, demanded Luther's renunciation of self and the world. Luther defied his father's wishes, renouncing a legal career, turning his back upon the increasingly secular environment of sixteenth-century Germany and in pursuit of a gracious God, entered the Augustinian monastery at Erfurt in 1505. But, in time, in Bonhoeffer's words, "Luther had to leave the cloister and go back to the world, not because the world in itself was good and holy, but because even the cloister was only a part of the world. . . . The renunciation he made when he became a monk was child's play compared with that which he had to make when he returned to the world."[74] When self-denial intends to answer the call of God, God is pleased. But the call to be separate from the world must prepare disciples to "go into the world" as witnesses.

Dogmatism

The underground seminary Bonhoeffer led at Finkenwalde served those churches that rejected the dominance and influence of the "German Christians" within the Lutheran church who were collaborating with Hitler's Third Reich. These "rebel" churches were called the "Confessing Church" because, in the words of the Barmen Declaration, they "confessed" certain evangelical truths including that "Jesus Christ, as he is attested to us in Holy Scripture, is the one Word of God whom we have to hear, and whom we have to trust and obey in life and in death."[75] Karl Barth, the principle author of this momentous document, shaped Bonhoeffer's thinking more profoundly than any other theologian. Bonhoeffer had briefly been Barth's student and colleague, and, as we have seen, Barth was able to offer assistance to Bonhoeffer after he had joined the resistance movement in Germany.

Barth's theology and life combined dimensions often seen as antithetical—the confessional and the practical, the dogmatic and the engaged, the quest for truth and the quest for relevance. Barth's stamp upon Bonhoeffer's life and thinking stand out at this point. The dogmatic element displays itself in various ways. Bonhoeffer insisted that the burden of the one who preaches the Bible is not to make the text relevant for contemporary hearers but rather to demonstrate how irrelevant we have become in our rebellion against the God revealed in Holy Scripture.

What does this mean—our irrelevance in the face of Scripture? Like Barth, Bonhoeffer begins and ends his search for the truth about God and humanity, about the church and the world, with the Bible. Rather than putting our questions to Scripture, the Christian willingly exposes himself to God's Word for scrutiny and judgment. Theology and ethics begin not with our questions for God but with God's for us. When Bonhoeffer encourages the questioning of Scripture, he means neither the projection of our values and hopes upon the text nor the subjection of the Bible to our judgment but rather the persistent pursuit of God's truth. For Barth, and then for Bonhoeffer, the quest for relevance demanded precisely such dogmatism in which truth is found outside of both the world and oneself in God's Word, where not only the right answers reside but the relevant questions as well.

Bonhoeffer gave intense attention to exegesis of biblical texts at the underground seminary at Finkenwalde and led his students to do the same. The German word typically translated into English as *presentation* means "to make present" or "to make relevant." Thus, when German pastors attempted the "presentation" of a text, they thought of making it present or relevant. Keeping this etymological nuance in mind, note Bonhoeffer's instructions to his would-be pastors at Finkenwalde:

> In principle, it is possible to interpret the question of
> the presentation of New Testament messages in two ways.
> The phrase means either that the biblical message must jus-
> tify itself to the present age and in that way must show itself
> capable of being made present, or that the present age must
> justify itself before the biblical message and in that way the
> message must become present. Where the question of pre-
> sentation is put with that uncanny urgency that we know so
> well, indeed is the central question of theology, it is always
> bound to serve the first purpose. The New Testament is
> meant to justify itself to the present age.[76]

Here Bonhoeffer assumes awareness of the lay of the land among university-trained expositors of Holy Scripture. The first task confronting the preacher demands not the "making relevant" of the ancient biblical text for the twentieth-century hearer.

What he found in the Bible was not a pitiful God whose lordship over the world was in question but the crucified, risen, and ascended Christ whose lordship was established and in effect. The task of the church was not one of establishment of Christ's lordship but of witness, proclamation, and obedience. The Scriptures call for witness to the now-enthroned Christ and proclamation of his present and coming reign together with all the promises attending his disciples. The Bible calls for obedience to the commands of the one Lord of this world.

Whatever else Bonhoeffer meant by the Christian worldliness appropriate to the church's witness, it had nothing to do with giving up the dogmatic, revelatory function of Holy Scripture. The God of the Old and New Testaments neither requires nor seeks validation from the world. Rather, the world, having rebelled against God, stands under divine judgment. The prophetic function of Christian proclamation continues to shape church responsibility in our world.

Certainly Bonhoeffer valued the removal of unnecessary stumbling blocks to the gospel in his day. But he just as certainly would have recoiled at the flight from such central teachings as the confession of sin and repentance as we see among many evangelicals today. Likewise Bonhoeffer's recognition of the exclusive claims of Christ as the only Savior and Lord of this world appear utterly incompatible with the pluralistic emphasis that shapes the politically correct spirituality of our day. For Bonhoeffer felt relevance does not define truth; truth defines true relevance. Where a gap exists, felt relevance and true relevance, revelation and repentance are called for, not adjustment of the biblical message.

In our world, where political correctness would enforce tolerance of diversity in matters of religion even within a confessional community, Bonhoeffer's confessional dogmatism may appear conspicuously Neanderthal:

A doctrine may be tolerated in one Church and proscribed in another (Rev. 2:6, 15ff). But once a heresy has become an open scandal it must of necessity be proscribed. The heretical teacher must be excommunicated and all personal intercourse with him avoided (Gal. 1:8; 1 Cor. 16:22; Titus 3:10; 2 John 10ff). The word of pure proclamation must visibly bind and loose. The space which the Church claims for its proclamations and order is thus made clear as an ordinance of divine appointment.[77]

Bonhoeffer the Fundamentalist?

Adolf von Harnack, the premier church historian of his generation and arguably representing something of an apex in the history of Protestant liberalism, was also the next-door neighbor to the Bonhoeffers. Harnack chafed at how smitten Bonhoeffer had become with Karl Barth and the obvious influence the Swiss theologian's theology was having on this young rising star in Berlin. He warned Bonhoeffer of the threat to spiritual life represented by contempt for scientific theology and the menace to it represented by unscientific theology. Those who hold high the flag of real science must therefore stand by it more steadfastly than ever. Barth's insistence that theology is indeed scientific on its own terms appealed to the young Bonhoeffer. Theology, when it stands on its own two feet, need not abandon the wider world of the sciences, but it should deny the prerogative of other sciences to impose tests and strictures upon theology that ignore the unique character of her object.

The object of Christian theology is God revealed in Jesus Christ, as witnessed to in Holy Scripture. Any serious quest for knowledge of this God must, as in all science, even physics, adjust itself to the character of the thing studied. If contemporary science lacks tools conducive to such study of this God, this should be admitted. What must be resisted is the denial that the church possesses such epistemological tools. The object of Christian theology is unique, and so the investigation of God will necessarily adjust to that uniqueness. Where areas of investigation overlap with common "secular" areas of inquiry, such as in say, archaeology, very well! We can dig together. But where unbelievers find themselves lacking, say, concerning the substitutionary atonement of Christ, very well! Admit as much, but do not then insist upon the irrationality of that quest for knowledge by others.

Bonhoeffer's attraction to Barth went well beyond the intellectual. Barth's theology had erupted out of the demand for preaching and pastoral labor and saw itself first of all as thinking in service to the church with all its pressing daily requirements. Bonhoeffer's own bent toward the concrete and the practical welcomed such a living theology. But, like Barth, the practical interest did not concern itself first of all with the felt relevance of the audience but with the truth of Holy Scripture and confidence that this pursuit led ultimately to true relevance.

Bonhoeffer repeatedly resisted direction and pressure from his early mentors to pursue an exclusively academic career in the area of history or ethics. Instead, Bonhoeffer doggedly took on heavy burdens as a working minister while investing his scholarly attention to systematic theology. Bonhoeffer wanted to say something as a working minister. For all his keen attention to the culture and the world in all its concreteness, Bonhoeffer was convinced that truth is relevant and that true Christianity offers nothing to the world if not its special message embodied in the cross of Jesus Christ.

The word *doctrine* once had the power to evoke strong passions one way or another. Today, facing politically correct insistence upon pluralism and a make-your-own-spirituality-as-you-go atmosphere, doctrine has been reduced to irrelevance for many evangelicals. Ostensibly born-again Bible believers who share the popular equation of religious liberty with doctrinal apathy are not hard to find. Within such a context this passage from Bonhoeffer's *Cost of Discipleship* must jar the sensibilities of many:

Of all the offices of the Church, the uncorrupted ministry of the Word and Sacraments is of paramount importance. . . . the aim of proclamation is always the same—namely, healthy and wholesome doctrine (2 Tim. 4.3; 1 Tim. 1.10; 4.16; 6.1; Titus 1.9, 13; 2.1; 3.8), and the guarantee of true order and unity.

It is not always easy to see where a legitimate school of thought ends and heresy begins. That is why a doctrine may be tolerated in one Church and proscribed in another (Rev. 2.6, 15 ff.). But once a heresy has become an open scandal it must of necessity be proscribed. The heretical teacher must be excommunicated, and all personal intercourse with him avoided (Gal. 1.8; 1 Cor. 16.22; Titus 3.10; 2 John 10ff).[78]

Liberal and progressive commentators on Bonhoeffer have found little use for such passages within the Bonhoeffer corpus even though their presence is conspicuous. But many evangelicals have paid a dear price for the loss of what we have called the dogmatic element so prominent in Bonhoeffer's thinking. We have in mind his concern for faithfulness to the Bible and concern for truth and doctrine. It is ironic that the erosion of and now amnesia regarding doctrine and truth among evangelicals has coincided with visible, widespread reclaiming and reassertion of inerrancy and the authority of the Bible among large numbers of evangelicals. It the case of the Southern Baptist Convention, the largest Protestant denomination in America, this recovery of the Bible, at least in a formal, confessional sense, has been nothing less than spectacular.

Many evangelicals have long insisted upon a correspondence between the extraordinary decline of the mainline Protestant denominations and their equivocation on biblical authority. Stop believing, stop evangelizing. Stop evangelizing, stop growing. Once a bad conscience regarding proselytizing takes hold, forget about church growth. People do not need to join and invest in communities of faith only to be told that they can pretty much believe and live as they choose and be saved along pretty much any path that suits them. In such an atmosphere, attraction to gospel ministry, not to mention missionary zeal, tends to evaporate.

From their seventeenth-century British beginnings, Baptists have displayed zeal for both truth and souls. Arguably, the twentieth century has witnessed the waning of doctrinal seriousness in favor of the evangelistic impulse. The utterly commendable hunger for souls has arguably outrun and contributed to the neglect of truth. My hunch is that the cultural and sociological conditions conducive to the marginalizing, neglect, and even outright abandonment of doctrine identified by David Wells accounts for these developments as well as any other obvious explanation. Surveys by veteran religious pollster George Barna make clear that, among evangelicals, the doctrinal center has not held.

Christ the Center

Bonhoeffer identified the epistemological source of Christian thinking and acting as Holy Scripture. But what did he find there? The short answer is, Jesus Christ. The God of Abraham, Isaac, and Jacob has revealed himself fully and finally by taking on humanity in Jesus Christ. Thus Bonhoeffer felt free to search for and find Jesus Christ in the Old Testament as well as the New. In the New Testament, Jesus Christ, both God and man, reveals God to man. The church must define itself with reference to Jesus Christ, and individual believers must do the same.

In Jesus Christ the world is confronted with a new humanity, which is also true humanity. This new humanity reveals itself first of all in the atoning work of Jesus Christ in which God, by letting himself be rejected and pushed out of the world by those he came to save, takes upon himself the sins of the world. Those who are called come to Jesus Christ in repentance and faith and are incorporated into the body of Christ, the church, wherein they participate in this new collective humanity established and maintained by Jesus Christ. Jesus Christ makes himself present to his disciples only within this divinely established fellowship, in the power of the Holy Spirit. Having been incorporated into this forgiven and redeemed fellowship, believers find themselves free from the egocentricity that had held them hostage. No longer must they live for themselves, defend themselves, demand their rights, and compete with others.

No longer must they imagine that their standing before God depends upon anything in themselves. They find themselves clothed with a righteousness not their own, the righteousness of Jesus Christ. They find themselves recipients of the promise of eternal life, heirs of Jesus Christ; having been buried with him through baptism, they are promised a resurrection like his. Thus they find themselves free to live for him. This life in him expresses itself first of all as a living for their brothers and sisters in Christ within the church, being built up in love. Then, as disciples of Christ who is Lord over all, they are free to live under his lordship within the world as his witnesses and, like him, prepared to suffer rejection at the hands of the world if necessary.

The incarnation of the Word of God in Jesus Christ together with the humiliation of the God-man on the cross, his resurrection and promised return in glory, is God's final word to the church. The church's speech and action in the world looks for its legitimacy as it reflects Jesus Christ. As such, this speech and action will declare

God's forgiveness and love through a preaching, suffering, loving, and hopeful church. Far from any temptation to retreat from the world, the church will claim the world as the legitimate sphere for obedience to its Lord, the Lord of this world, Jesus Christ.

Worldly Christianity

Certainly some of the most enigmatic and even shocking of Bonhoeffer's statements surrounded what he called, negatively, "religionless Christianity," and, positively, "worldly Christianity." One dimension of Bonhoeffer's concern was to distinguish, along the lines of Barth, between true Christianity and "religion" as such. If religion results, as Ludwig von Feuerbach had argued, from the projection of humanity's own highest hopes, dreams, and fantasies into the metaphysical realm, then Christianity is no religion. God in Christ confronts sinful humanity with a new and strange word of judgment and grace. This message comes down from God, not up from man. Thus the gospel of Jesus Christ is revelation in the strict sense. In the face of this revelation, man finds himself not affirmed but judged, called to repentance, forgiven, adopted as God's child, set within the body of Christ, called to bear witness to Christ, and destined for eternal life.

Religionless Christianity also meant the renunciation of self-justification. Bonhoeffer took from Luther a strong aversion to all works of righteousness and an equally strong protectiveness of the grace character of true discipleship. Sinners saved by grace live from and under the forgiveness of sins.

A more significant use of the terms "religionless Christianity" and "worldly Christianity" took quite a different, if not opposite and contradictory, direction. Here Bonhoeffer grappled with the advance of secular thinking and culture in which humanity turns less and less to revelation or God for answers to its questions or help with its diffi-culties. Instead, secular man thinks for himself, accepts responsibility for himself and the world, and so tackles problems on his own. In such an environment God is largely ignored; and if God is considered at all, it is as a stopgap, providing answers to questions beyond the reach of humanity's current tools. God is brought in as the *deus ex machina* of the Greek theater, to solve problems otherwise intractable.

As the so-called frontiers of knowledge are pushed back, so then is God. God is relegated to the margins of life, his relevance shrink-ing to the vanishing point. Bonhoeffer is often read as accepting the competence of the world in its pretentious advancing of the frontiers of knowledge. This is a mistake. Bonhoeffer lamented the retreat of the church in the face of the world's increasing secularization. Christ is the Lord of the world whether the world acknowledges this lordship or not. The believer, however, does acknowledge this lordship and so may and must plunge into the center of the world, taking upon himself the struggles and sufferings of the world in the name of Jesus Christ rather than accepting the world's ignoring of God or relegation of the Christ to the margins of life. No! Christ is present right in the center of life, and his lordship should be recognized and submitted to there. By joining the conspiracy to assassinate Adolf Hitler, Bonhoeffer was attempting just such a submission to Christ's lordship at the center of life in this world.

When he spoke of worldly Christianity, Bonhoeffer never had in mind assimilation of the gospel message to the world or to culture but the opposite. He called for a critical grappling with, understanding of, and resistance to the rise of secularism. He decried the invasion of secular modes of thought within the church, viewing such assimila-tion as the corrupting absorption of worldliness, whether conscious or not, as a cancer in the church.

Bonhoeffer's allegiance to the Bible did not transfer to tradition. Like some of the more prominent leaders within the church growth movement, Bonhoeffer recognized the need for new language by which to communicate the gospel and its demands in an increasingly secular world. Responsible for the instruction of poor and working class children within communities long devoid not only of Christianity but religion of any kind, Bonhoeffer set aside the catechism with its traditional formulations. The language of Zion might as well have been Chinese to these young people.

Still Bonhoeffer had no penchant for innovation for its own sake; clear communication of the gospel was what mattered. In contrast to many iconoclastic by-passers of Christian tradition today, Bonhoeffer was steeped in his own tradition and appreciated its historic guidance and usefulness. But its continued usefulness depended on its power to proclaim the gospel to the world and to believers today, not yesterday.

Dogmatism is retained in Bonhoeffer's use of tradition. Conveyance of truth, in both language and action, authenticates the gospel, rather than any independent appeal to felt relevance. Bonhoeffer remained enough of a Barthian to recognize the inevitably idolatrous character of relevance-driven theologizing. Such conviction did not render relevance unimportant. It did mean that relevance authenticated itself according to the revelation of God in Holy Scripture, not according to the self-diagnoses of sinful humanity. The God revealed in Jesus Christ not only prescribes medicine and treatment for a sin-sick world but handles the diagnoses as well.

When seen in the context of his Barthian dogmatism, Bonhoeffer's call for a religionless Christianity must be seen as a quest for the recovery of true Christianity and of the true church, not their abandonment or abolition as some have argued. Supposed compatibility between Bonhoeffer's thinking and the death of God theology that sometimes claimed inspiration from him is an illusion. It is true that Bonhoeffer expected his participation in the conspiracy to assassinate Hitler to disqualify him from the ordained ministry should he survive. It is also true that Bonhoeffer believed and hoped that it was precisely obedience to Christ that compelled his conspiratorial activity. What this seeming contradiction reveals is not the incompatibility of true discipleship with church-based Christianity but rather Bonhoeffer's respect for the prerogative of the church to pass judgment on his actions together with Bonhoeffer's doubt that even the Confessing Church was yet able to see matters as clearly as he did. Given this circumstance, Bonhoeffer was prepared to accept the prophet's reward.

Ministry

In 1929, having plunged himself exclusively into academic work, Bonhoeffer's love for ministry and fellowship with ordinary Christians reasserted itself along with his commitment to rigorous scholarly endeavor: "Soon I shall be going to Barcelona for a fortnight's visit to my [former] congregation, of which I am very fond, and I feel in general that academic work will not hold me for long. On the other hand, I think it very important to have as thorough an academic grounding as possible."[79] This statement fairly exposes the function of the two inner passions of Bonhoeffer's life, namely that, for him at least, academic work must serve hands-on ministry.

Toward the end of his life, Bonhoeffer insisted that he stood by what he wrote in *The Cost of Discipleship* while conceding that he would have to say things a little differently now. I contend that the difference concerns the goal of the Christian life. *The Cost of Discipleship*, despite its strong embrace of self-denial and sacrifice, nevertheless retained something of that personal quest to "be something" before others and God. Bonhoeffer came to reject every shred of such personal concern as a betrayal of grace, which in turn threatened to alter the character of the Christian life itself. Bonhoeffer's growing appreciation for Christ's completed work on the cross heightened his protectiveness for life under the grace of God. These convictions turned on the identification of the one who died on Calvary:

> Everything depends on whether one thinks that Jesus Christ is the idealistic founder of a religion or the very Son of God. Nothing less than the life and death of the human being hangs in the balance. If he was the idealistic founder of a religion, then I can be inspired by his accomplishments and motivated to imitate his zeal, but my sin is not forgiven. In this instance God is still very angry with me, and I am under the power of death. Jesus' work leads me in this case to total despair about myself.
>
> If however, the work of Christ is the work of God, then I am not summoned to act like God or imitate God zealously, but instead I am convicted by this work as one who in no way can do it by myself. Rather I have found all at once the gracious God through this Jesus Christ, in this knowledge and in this work. My sin has been forgiven. I am not dead but alive. It depends therefore on the person of Christ, whether his work is understood as passing away according to the old world of death or whether it is eternal according to a new world of life.[80]

How politically incorrect this excerpt must fall upon progressive ears today. This is straight Lutheran orthodoxy. As far as the nature of discipleship is concerned, take note especially of this phrase, "I am not summoned to act like God or to imitate God zealously."[81] Bonhoeffer did not reject all notions of imitation in discipleship, and he did point to Christ as a model for believers, particularly in so far as suffering must belong to the disciple's lot. But Bonhoeffer recognized that viable imitation of Christ depends utterly upon recognition of the way in which he can never be our model, namely, as the crucified God-man who bears the sins of the world on the cross.

When the slightest drop of works righteousness seeps into the disciple's motivation for obedience, belief in Jesus Christ has given way to unbelief. In its wake a perhaps unconscious, yet not less deadly, futile and sinful attempt at imitation ensues. The sinner saved by grace now would save himself. The sinner made righteous by the cross would make himself righteous by obedience.

Bonhoeffer's orthodox and Protestant Christianity shines forth here. All the supposed necessary incentives to right living viewed as so necessary within other religions and to false Christianity are rejected. Disciples live from the confrontation with the crucified and risen Savior who has indeed borne the punishment for sin, nailing it to the cross. Motivation to obedience cannot come from a desire to put ourselves right with God because that has been accomplished, and no creeping doubts or sideways glances to our continuing sinfulness can undo what Christ has done. Motivation now arises as response to the cross and resurrection, gratitude to God, belief in his promises, and embracing of his ways.

Service Versus Introspection

Two days after the Allied invasion at Normandy, in a letter to Eberhard Bethge, Bonhoeffer reflected on the introspective fixation of much contemporary theology from his cell in Tegel prison:

> We have now the secularized offshoots of Christian theology, namely the existentialists philosophy and the psychotherapists, who demonstrate to secure, contented, and happy mankind that it is really unhappy and desperate and simply unwilling to admit that it is in a predicament about which it knows nothing, and from which only they can rescue it. Wherever there is health, strength, security, simplicity, they scent luscious fruit to gnaw at or to lay their pernicious eggs in. They set themselves to drive people to inward despair, and then the game is in their hands. That is secularized Methodism. And whom does it touch? A small number of intellectuals, of degenerates, of people who regard themselves as the most important thing in the world, and who therefore like to busy themselves with themselves. The ordinary man, who spends his everyday life at work with his family, and of course with all kinds of diversions, is not affected. He has neither the time nor the inclination to concern himself with his existential despair, or to regard his perhaps modest share of happiness as a trial, or a trouble, or a calamity.[82]

Key insights into the heart of Bonhoeffer's faith become visible in this extraordinary passage, composed just ten months before his execution. First, we see a young scholar refusing to allow prison bars to separate him from his vocation as a theologian in service to the church. We see also how keenly he perceived and felt the effects of what he considered bad theology for the ordinary believer. Perhaps most forcefully, we see his intolerance for theology that encourages a cloying preoccupation with one's own plight to the abandonment of responsibility for others, service to the world, and witness to Jesus Christ.

Keep in mind that this same Dietrich Bonhoeffer spoke fervently for a Christian discipleship bound to the world in all its triumph and tragedy, a discipleship ready to enter into the struggles and hurts of others even to the pouring out of one's own life. And yet he recoiled against any pursuit of self-fulfillment or other forms of self-preoccupation as ends in themselves. One expects that Bonhoeffer would have welcomed the opening line of Rick Warren's *The Purpose Driven Life*—"It's not about you!"[83] That Bonhoeffer would have shared the reticence to offer prophetic calls to repentance regarding abortion or homosexual behavior seems unlikely.

Perhaps the most convicting prophetic dimension of Bonhoeffer's life and work for us today emerges precisely in his call for self-denying preoccupation with the concerns of others, of the community, and of the world. At some level Bonhoeffer's sustained attractiveness among Christians has little to do with any new word or fresh insight but with an old word we recognize from our acquaintance with the Bible or better, our acquaintance with Jesus Christ himself. Could it be that the mark of authenticity we encounter in Bonhoeffer finally reduces to the call of Jesus to self-denying sacrifice and love? Could it be that what we encounter in Bonhoeffer is nothing less than the call to repentance we could have found in the New Testament?

Insofar as Bonhoeffer's willingness to die in obedience to the command of his Lord appears to us new and strange, so our guilt is exposed and our need for repentance is intensified. From one perspective Bonhoeffer's life and work might be best understood as a simple recovery of the gospel and of a biblical conception of discipleship in the face of great efforts in our own day to transform Christianity into one more competing strategy for human happiness. Could it be that, as believers in Christ, we recognize that true happiness for us can only come as we are freed from the direct pursuit of happiness as such? Do we not retain at least the memory that only service to others, witness to Jesus Christ, and obedience to the commands of our Savior offer peace for us who have been purchased by the blood of Jesus?

Does not our encounter with Bonhoeffer remind us of Jesus' insistence that only those who lose their lives for his sake save them? Rather than cloister himself from the demands of church life, Bonhoeffer took on heavy ministerial duties just when he faced the daunting demands of doctoral research. He gave weekly guidance to Sunday school teachers in the preparation of their lessons. In addition Bonhoeffer accepted responsibility for catechizing a group of children at Grunewald, investing in their lives beyond the call of duty, organizing special outings for them, and having them in his home frequently for games and music and meals. Friends from Bonhoeffer's intellectual circle warned him that the social gap between himself, his message, and those he ministered to posed insuperable barriers to enduring relevance and relationship. Such nay-saying only emboldened Bonhoeffer, leaving him determined to test his theology and ethics in actual ministry. For him "the theological pronouncements of Barth were worth nothing if they could not be explained *in toto* to these Grunewald children."[84]

Many aspiring scholars pursuing the doctorate chafed at the ministry requirement then prevailing at Berlin and found ways to check off the ministry box as quickly and painlessly as possible. Not Bonhoeffer. Once his catechetical students outgrew the Sunday class, Bonhoeffer started a Thursday reading and discussion group in order to maintain his ministry among them. Papers on religious, historical, economic, and political subjects were presented by Bonhoeffer. They enjoyed field trips together, spending hours together during which these youth, many from Jewish families including several atheists, would speak their minds and challenge their teacher who patiently answered their questions. Many of these students continued to correspond with Bonhoeffer across the years. Nearly all of these students would die in Hitler's war or in the concentration camps, as would their kind teacher.

On December 17, 1927, the twenty-year-old Bonhoeffer defended his doctoral thesis at Berlin, being awarded the rare *summa cum laude*. Bonhoeffer's parents and teachers fully expected the now certifiably brilliant Dietrich to pursue the academic career open to him, but it was not to be. Little did they realize that Bonhoeffer's internal struggle was not to attain to the academic life but to escape from it. The pulpit, not the lectern, beckoned. In February 1928 Bonhoeffer arrived in Barcelona to assume duties as an assistant pastor to a congregation of German expatriates. Bonhoeffer found the contrast between Spain and Grunewald jarring and disturbing as he sought to minister among his own countrymen with their "petty bourgeois outlook." But the experience only confirmed and fueled his conviction that true Christianity must be lived out, not only thought through, and it must center upon witness to Christ in the midst of offering genuine, concrete help to others. In Bonoeffer's mind this aim of a true disciple contrasts most obviously with self-centeredness, ambition, the yearning to "be something" for oneself. Where such self-interest characterizes the believer's passions, so the refusal to "get one's hands dirty" by plunging into the tempest of life takes hold. The context where true discipleship should shine forth appears as a threat to the quest for holiness in the mind of the spiritually inward. Bonhoeffer's convictions on such matters intensified and no doubt stifled his resolve as his entanglement within the resistance to Hitler deepened. The following excerpt from his *Ethics* dates from 1942:

> Because Jesus is not about the proclamation and realization of new ethical ideals, nor about his own moral purity, but only about love for real human beings, therefore he is able to enter into communion with their guilt. . . . Out of his selfless love and his sinlessness, Jesus enters into the guilt of humanity, taking it upon himself. . . . Whoever wants to escape from responsibility for guilt withdraws . . . from the redeeming mystery of Jesus Christ's sinless guilt offering and has no share in the divine justification, which is based on this event. Someone like this puts personal innocence over responsibility for humanity and is blind to the enormous guilt that is thereby taken upon oneself.[85]

Nationalism and Witness

Bonhoeffer came to recognize and resist the dangerous corrosive potential of nationalism within the church. Where loyalty to the state figures prominently within the self-consciousness of the disciple or of the church, the propensity for compromise of the gospel and betrayal of Jesus Christ also rises. It is not as though the church cares nothing for or owes nothing to the state. Quite to the contrary. Bonhoeffer never doubted the lordship of Christ, not only over the church but also over the state. The church in fact recognizes the proper sphere of the state, including the duty to reward the good and punish the bad. The church, however, owes the state the prophetic proclamation of the gospel together with warning of God's judgment should the state fail in its biblically demarcated responsibilities.

These convictions should not be associated with, say, a kind of blame-America-first reflex now prominent among some political liberals who promote exactly the sort of secularizing agenda Bonhoeffer abhorred. But his views do sound a warning to any Christian church tied too closely to any particular political party. The independent prophetic office of the church vis-à-vis the state is a precious duty to be protected and employed in service to both God and the world. As Southern Baptist Richard Land has insisted, followers of Jesus Christ should vote values, not party.

Dimensions of Witness

For Bonhoeffer, witness identifies the heart of the church's task vis-à-vis the world. Witness must include both speech and action, word and deed. Bonhoeffer identified three ways the church should relate to the governments. First, the church must declare the biblically revealed responsibility of the state. The church has a prophetic role as God's messenger to admonish and warn where the state fails to reward the good, punish wrongdoing, and maintain justice according to biblical teachings.

The church must also come to the aid of the victims of government misconduct and atrocity insofar as it is capable. When Bonhoeffer participated in Operation 7, by which Jews were smuggled into Switzerland, he sought to fulfill a duty of Christian witness. Nevertheless, witness to Jesus Christ demands more than offering aid and comfort to victims; it demands resistance to government crimes. Note that Bonhoeffer reasons from a dogmatic position at this point. The church looks not to the state itself or to history or to natural law in order to identify what might constitute government misconduct or injustice but to Holy Scripture. And while the threshold for the justification of active resistance to the state is set high, that threshold can be reached. For Bonhoeffer, Hitler's reign of terror cleared the threshold.

Despite his two statements to the contrary, Bonhoeffer seems not to have maintained an utterly clear conscience regarding his conspiratorial activity. Perhaps a more accurate grasp of his situation would be to say that he could not maintain a good conscience remaining apart from the resistance and eventually the conspiracy itself once opportunity to join presented itself. Once again we meet with Bonhoeffer's preference for bold yet humble, non-self-justifying thrusts "into the tempest of living" over against an overweening moral fastidiousness more interested in maintaining an abstract purity than in addressing wrong and suffering while there is still time. Better to get one's hands dirty and cling to the forgiveness purchased on the cross than sit idly while unbelievers and other "worldly" folk expose themselves to imprisonment, torture, and death to achieve something Christians would welcome and enjoy the fruit of should success be achieved.

Bonhoeffer grew increasingly confident that the third task of the church vis-à-vis the state—resistance—must be recognized. Once, distinguishing the second and third tasks, Bonhoeffer insisted that church must not only "bandage the victims under the wheel [of state injustice] but put a spoke in the wheel itself."

The Confessing Church and the Barmen Declaration

Bonhoeffer would eventually find himself caught up in the conspiracy to assassinate Hitler. It is not true that Bonhoeffer's decision to do so was preceded by a long period of research, agonizing, and prayer at the end of which he moved with utter certainty into the conspiracy, prepared to defend himself against all detractors. Time did not allow for the luxury of such deliberation and the achievement of a completely clear conscience. But what is true is that, ideally, Bonhoeffer valued reflection and dialogue, and he certainly considered the use of force against an enemy as a last resort. The clearest attempt by the Confessing Church to state its position and head off a tragic collision with Hitler came in the form of a confessional statement drafted in May 1934 by a group of pastors and especially under the influence of Bonhoeffer's teacher/mentor, Karl Barth.

Following the victory of the Hitler-friendly German Christians in the church elections held on July 23, 1933, Bonhoeffer, together with Professor Hermann Sasse of Erlangen, edited a first draft of what became know as the "Bethel Confession." The following excerpt from a letter to his grandmother during his work on the confession reveals something of the purpose of the confession but also Bonhoeffer's pessimism and determination to see the truth exposed:

> We want to try to make the German Christians declare their intentions. Whether we shall succeed I rather doubt. For even if they admit the formulations officially, the pressure behind them is so strong that sooner or later it is bound to sweep away all promises. It is becoming increasingly clear that what we are going to get is a big, popular, national church whose nature cannot be reconciled with Christianity, and that we must be prepared to enter upon entirely new paths which we shall then have to tread. The real question is between Germanism and Christianity, and the sooner the conflict comes into the open the better. Nothing could be more dangerous than its concealment.[86]

The Bethel Confession became the precursor to the Barmen Declaration which, in turn, became the enduring confessional basis and explanation for the intractable conflict to come.

Bonhoeffer joined with others who were likewise convinced of the seriousness of the threat posed by Hitler's Nazi regime. The emerging political situation threatened not only the Jews but the church as well. In the face of the attempted usurpation of the church's prerogatives of self-governance, defense of the gospel itself was demanded. Witness to Jesus Christ in such circumstances must be clear, formal, and public. Accordingly, Bonhoeffer found himself at the forefront of new "confessional" demands. Particularly under the leadership of Swiss theologian Karl Barth, the so-called "Confessing Church" crafted and adopted the Barmen Confession, taking its stand against Hitler's encroachments into the proper sphere of the church.

Hitler's rise to power in January 1933 precipitated a crisis for the churches of Germany. The church was to be "coordinated" with the three main doctrines of National Socialism—nationalism, racism, and militarism. Bonhoeffer's ecumenical activity is better understood as a quest for confessional seriousness by the international church over against "the world" than for a kind doctrinal latitudinarianism that too often characterizes ecumenism in our day.

By that summer the Aryan paragraph adopted by the so-called German Christians prohibited Jews or anyone married to "non-Aryans" from serving as ministers. In May 1934, at Barmen, a new confession, drafted by Karl Barth, "fortified by strong coffee and one or two Brazilian cigars" reasserted the Reformation solus Christus and sola Scriptura in the face of Nazism.[87] The document represented a throwback to Reformation and patristic creeds and confessions, replete with clear affirmations, rejections, and anathemas.

While Bonhoeffer himself could not be at Barmen, he worked tirelessly for its production, adoption, and dissemination. The Barmen Declaration marks the fulfillment of a dream for Bonhoeffer and represents a striking example of Christian witness so prized by him. As his biographer and close friend Eberhard Bethge noted, "The Barmen Synod had proclaimed and enacted what [Bonhoeffer] had long been putting forward as the criterion of his word and deeds."[88] As a window into the profound confessional character of Bonhoeffer's conception of witness within the world, we will take a close look at the Barmen Declaration produced by the synod of the same name.

Considering the disproportionate welcome Bonhoeffer has received among progressivist Christians, the confessional dogmatism and politically incorrect content of Barmen is conspicuous. Article 1 reads:

> I am the Way and the Truth and the Life; no one comes to the Father except through me (John 14:6). Truly, truly, I say to you, whoever does not enter the sheepfold through the door, but climbs in somewhere else, that one is a thief and a robber. I am the Door; anyone who enters through me will be saved (John 10:1, 9). Jesus, as he is attested to us in Holy Scripture, is the one Word of God whom we have to hear, and whom we have to trust and obey in life and in death. We reject the false doctrine that the church could and should recognize as a source of its proclamation, beyond and besides this one Word of God, yet other events, powers, historic figures, and truths as God's revelation.[89]

At once we find in these words the clear and blunt affirmation of the historic, exclusive claims of Christianity for the Bible as its source and authority and Jesus Christ as the sole means of salvation for sinful humanity. Given such conviction, allegiance is reserved solely to the Word of God as attested in Jesus Christ according to the Scriptures. The concluding rejection of false doctrine related to other competing sources of revelation exposes a deep, ongoing struggle within the church over the legitimacy and role of natural theology. The immediate occasion for this "rejection" was Hitler's own claim that the ideology of National Socialism being advanced by the Nazi Party within the Third Reich be recognized as a new divine revelation. Hitler demanded that the new "insights" of National Socialism be accepted as binding on a par with the revelation in Holy Scripture. Eventually it became clear that Hitler's plan involved not a blending of the cross and the swastika but the displacement of the former by the latter. In the end there would be room for only one revelation, that of the Nazis.

At some level Barth must have relished this opportunity to unleash his own churning revulsion against natural theology upon such a heinous, concrete target as Adolf Hitler provided. Within a year he would respond to fellow Swiss theologian Emil Brunner's booklet entitled "Natural Theology" with a tract of his own bearing perhaps the shortest theological title in history—"N*ein!*" (No!).[90]

What was this natural theology underlying the first "rejection" of the confession, and what danger did it pose to the church in the minds of Barmen's supporters? The history of the natural theology had been infused with new vigor during the nineteenth century, not always or mostly as a part of an attempt to reject or dispense with the revelation of Holy Scripture but rather to recognize beside that ancient source other sources. Not only has the Bible revealed divine truth but also reason or conscience or history or emotion or nature itself. Often recognition of another or even multiple sources of divine revelation were brought in to confirm the Bible's own witness, if not to provide the epistemological props themselves. The knowability of God in Jesus

Christ was combined with the knowability of God in nature, reason, history, and so on.

In the Barmen Declaration, the church confesses that it knows but one Word of God, one Jesus Christ, its only Lord, its comfort, attested in Holy Scripture. It confesses no other Word, no other Jesus Christ, and finds no comfort elsewhere but here, in this one Word. It will not listen to a stranger however decked out with fancy and pretentious clothes borrowed from nature or reason or wherever. This church acknowledges and indeed rejoices at the legitimacy of any number of epistemologically viable sources of truth, including reason, conscience, emotion, history, and nature but only so long as they operate within their proper sphere. This church only recognizes idols outside the revelation of God in Jesus Christ attested in Holy Scripture. Wow! It is no wonder that Barth, before Bonhoeffer and with more intensity, was viewed as having lapsed into some kind of impressive, reactionary fundamentalism by his critics on the left. And Hitler provided the perfect opportunity to show how intertwined are natural theology and idol making.

Strictly speaking, neither Karl Barth nor the Barmen Declaration ruled out the possibility of a natural theology. But both recognize only one source for church proclamation—the Word of God, Jesus Christ, attested in Holy Scripture. Thus, article 1 protects the purity, the authenticity of church proclamation. In article 2, Barmen addresses the claim of its Lord upon its active life within the world:

> Jesus Christ has been made wisdom and righteousness and sanctification and redemption for us by God (1 Cor. 1:30).
>
> As Jesus Christ is God's comforting pronouncement for the forgiveness of all our sins, so, and with equal seriousness, he is also God's vigorous announcement of his claim upon our whole life. Through him there comes to us joyful liberation

from the godless ties of this world for free, grateful service to his creatures.

We reject the false doctrine that there could be areas of our life in which we would not belong to Jesus Christ but to other lords, areas in which we would not need justification and sanctification through him.[91]

In our day, ecumenical dialogue sometimes signals a willingness to compromise one's position for the sake of a suspect unity, often purchased at the price of doctrinal compromise on matters previously recognized as nonnegotiable tenets of one's faith. Such was not the case with Bonhoeffer, and Barmen's article 2 offers an opportunity to discover why. Notwithstanding Bonhoeffer's strong, typically Lutheran recognition of the state's divinely established prerogatives vis-à-vis the church (Rom. 13), the church must never cede its own prerogatives as servants of the Lord of both state and church. Furthermore, the state exists for the sake of the church and not the other way round. Thus, the church will not recognize the state as its lord in any area of its life, come what may. Should the state attempt to encroach upon the church's exclusive allegiance to the only lord it recognizes, article 1 makes clear that the church has the comfort needed in its own Lord, whom it must trust and obey in life and in death.

The authors of the earliest confessions of numerous denominations attempt first to rank themselves with other streams within the Christian tradition on fundamental matters before defining distinctive beliefs and practices of its own tradition. One effect of this procedure is to communicate to governments the fundamentally Christian, orthodox posture being taken by the confessors. Bonhoeffer saw ecumenical activity as a legitimate vehicle for demonstrating fundamental Christian thinking to the world and in this case to the Third Reich. Thus ecumenical activity represented a quest for the doctrinal purity and seriousness prerequisite to genuine unity, not doctrinal minimalism or compromise. Where ecumenical dialogue meets with success, ecumenical confession results and allows the church to demonstrate its transdenominational and even international solidarity over against all enemies of the church and its message.

The following excerpt from article 3 reveals the uncompromising protectiveness the church throughout the ages has demonstrated with regard to its message:

> With both its faith and its obedience, with both its message and its order, it has to testify in the midst of the sinful world, as the church of pardoned sinners, that it belongs to him alone and lives and may live by his comfort and under his direction alone, in expectation of his appearing.
>
> We reject the false doctrine that the church could have permission to hand over the form of its and of its order to whatever it itself might wish or to the vicissitudes of the prevailing ideological and political convictions of the day.[92]

Once again we see the dogmatic and politically incorrect posture Barth and Bonhoeffer and, at least for a period of time, the Confessing Church took over against the state and the world. The church points the state and the world to Jesus Christ as the only Lord, awaits his coming, and prepares itself to suffer if necessary rather than close its mouth in the face of opposition.

Article 5 delineates more specifically the church's understanding of the boundaries of state prerogative and responsibility:

> Scripture tells us that by divine appointment the state, in this still unredeemed world in which also the church is situated, has the task of maintaining justice and peace, so far as human discernment and human ability make this possible, by means of the threat and use of force. The church

acknowledges with gratitude and reverence toward God the benefit of this, his appointment. It draws attention to God's kingdom (*Reich*), God's commandment and justice and with these the responsibility of those who rule and those who are ruled. It trusts and obeys the power of the Word, by which God upholds all things.

We reject the false doctrine that beyond its special commission the state should and could become the sole and total order of human life and so fulfill the vocation of the church as well.

We reject the false doctrine that beyond its special commission the church should and could take on the nature, tasks and dignity which belong to the state and thus become itself organ of the state.[93]

Of course, Bonhoeffer, along with the framers of the Barmen Declaration, believed that the so-called "German Christians" within the German Evangelical Church had compromised its confession precisely along the lines rejected in the articles. The repudiation of that stance established the confessional basis of the Confessing Church within the German Evangelical Church and set itself on a collision course with Hitler's Third Reich. When the state refused to acknowledge the divinely appointed sphere of the church as witness to its Lord, it set Bonhoeffer on a collision course with the Fuehrer himself.

Bonhoeffer's Pacifism

The character of Bonhoeffer's pacifism has been a subject of controversy and is likely to remain so because here, as in so many cases, his thought was not developed to full maturity. Irresistibly, events drew him away from the kind of academic commitment he longed to pursue, thrusting him into the public arena where, in his case, decisions must be made without delay. And, of course, his life was cut short by the Nazis, who executed him a mere month after his thirty-ninth birthday.

Bonhoeffer's extant statements on the subject of pacifism present a sometimes confusing and even contradictory picture. They range from almost absolutist pronouncements in *Cost of Discipleship* (1937) through accepting the use of violence as a last resort (*ultima ratio*) in *Ethics* (1940) to zanily surprising antipacifist statements such as those appearing in an address to his congregation in Barcelona in 1929.

Besides demands for active ministerial and political work which limited Bonhoeffer's capacity to think through the issue as he might have liked, the issue of pacifism was also a neglected theme in Germany at that time. Thus, when Bonhoeffer called himself a pacifist, he found himself virtually alone. Even the Confessing Church opposed him. So how do we assess Bonhoeffer as a pacifist?

We should take note that, whatever he meant by the term, Bonhoeffer did call himself a pacifist as late as 1939. And the bulk of the Bonhoeffer corpus would seem to render his few early antipacifistic statements enigmatic. We can also recognize that the justification of tyrannicide, which Bonhoeffer obviously accepted in practice, need not lead to the justification of violence in warfare. However, efforts to draw such a distinction in Bonhoeffer's writings strike this writer as unimpressive. On the other hand, Bonhoeffer's participation in the conspiracy to assassinate Hitler would seem to prove that he permanently rejected the radical Christian pacifism of *Cost of Discipleship* (though some commentators attempt to reconcile *Cost of Discipleship* and *Ethics* according to typical Lutheran, two-sphere thinking). Without taking a dogmatic position, perhaps we can say that Bonhoeffer fairly consistently maintained a strong Christian aversion to the use of violence, accepting its inevitability only as a last resort. This still leaves aside the question of the criteria by which believers recognize whether last resort conditions are met.

What we can say with real confidence is that Bonhoeffer found retreat from the concrete problems of humankind on supposed Christian or theological grounds intolerable. Better to sin boldly and let grace abound (Luther) than to welcome and enjoy the benefits of Hitler's assassination by others while smugly adoring and displaying one's own ostensibly clean hands! Bonhoeffer's pacifism accepted agonizing participation in violence, asking for forgiveness all along the way but refusing to stand by and let nonbelievers do the dirty work.

War on Terror and Saddam Hussein

Bonhoeffer eventually reached the conclusion that his loyalty to Jesus Christ compelled him, at the risk of his own life, to join the conspiracy to assassinate Hitler. Why? In order to stop the torture and murder of innocent life, and in order to remove obstacles to a new and better future for Germany, should such a future become possible. How ought followers of Jesus Christ respond where governments torture and kill not because of anything someone has done, but merely because of who they are? And what would Bonhoeffer do? Should not good faith efforts to put a stop to torture and the murder of innocent life be admired?

It is not true that Bonhoeffer agonized over a long period of time and finally came to a position of conviction, if not utter certainty about the course of action he had to take. When he speaks of having a clear conscience about his participation in the conspiracy to assassinate Hitler, he means something akin to the abandonment of self-justification in the matter. He means that he offers his decision to

God for judgment. He means that he could no longer maintain a good conscience by attempting to keep his own hands "clean" while praying for the "success" of military and "secular" attempts to stop Hitler.

We cannot say for certain how Bonhoeffer would assess the overthrow of Saddam Hussien or efforts to stop Al Qaida, but certainly we are dealing here with similarly heinous and urgent matters of human atrocity. What does the legacy of Bonhoeffer's life and work have to say in the face of the targeting of innocents, the maintenance of rape rooms, torture chambers, and mass graves? I would suggest that the recognition of responsibility in such circumstances should lead to resistance and active opposition to the perpetrators of these crimes. Certainly, Bonhoeffer's designation of the Nazi regime as evil diverges from sanguine liberal assessments of human nature and the seemingly inexhaustible patience for discussion and pursuit of mutual understanding, or at best, the leveling of economic sanctions while thousands die and millions live in servile fear of the torture and execution of their loved ones and themselves.

Jean Bethke Elshtain found it difficult to reconcile Bonhoeffer's earlier and more radical pacifist statements with his later views and especially his actions:

> Dietrich Bonhoeffer, . . . writing as one dedicated to overthrowing Hitler, judged harshly those who retreated into the "sanctuary of private *virtuousness*," when confronted with hideous injustice. "Anyone who does this must shut his mouth and his eyes to the injustice around him," Bonhoeffer writes. "Responsible action" involves contamination—one cannot altogether avoid getting one's "hands dirty" when action in the political world in a responsible way. Bonhoeffer also criticized a "naïve lack of realism" on the part of the "reasonable" people whose failure, he argued,

"is obvious," since they believe, with "the best of intentions"
. . . that with a little reason they can bend back into position
the framework that has gotten out of joint.[94]

The use of force allowed in traditional just war theory would seem
to approximate Bonhoeffer's justification for joining the conspiracy to
assassinate Adolf Hitler fairly well. While I share Eberhard Bethge's
insistence that the Bonhoeffer corpus is characterized more by continuity than by development or sharp changes of direction, much
less reversals, I do not see how Bonhoeffer's actions, the rationale he
put forward in support of those actions, and the good conscience he
claimed in respect to them can be reconciled with the radical pacifism present in his early writings.

In any case, Christians today must face once again the question of resistance and the use of military force against tyranny in its
new form—international terrorism. I do not believe those calling for
restraint, patience, and understanding while innocents die and the
plotting of more murder continues apace can claim Bonhoeffer as a
guide.

Abortion

Bonhoeffer followed Luther in the view that God established
marriage for all humankind and thus not as a religious institution
in the first instance. Marriage involved the joining of one man and
one woman in covenantal union. While not ruling out the temporary
use of contraception, a marriage in which "the emergence of life is
consistently prevented, a marriage in which the desire for a child is
consistently excluded . . . is in contradiction to the meaning of marriage itself."[95] That is not to suggest that propagation of the race is the
only purpose of marriage. No one, according Bonhoeffer, held such a

narrow view before Immanuel Kant (1724–1804); such a view not only lacks support in Scripture but positively contradicts biblical teaching. What circumstances might justify the temporary use of contraceptives Bonhoeffer left up to the Christian conscience. He did clearly refuse to equate the use of contraceptives with abortion.

Bonhoeffer took a strong and conservative position on abortion. Destruction of the embryo in the mother's womb, he insisted, "is a violation of the right to live which God has bestowed upon this nascent life."[96] Once conception occurs, we know that "God certainly intended to create a human being," and should the fetus be aborted, we know that "this nascent human being has been deliberately deprived of his life. And that is nothing but murder."[97] Bonhoeffer recognized that the motives and circumstances leading to the decision to abort an unborn child vary greatly and that such a decision is sometimes taken out of great despair, human destitution, and so forth. He admitted that the circumstances surrounding the decision to seek an abortion should no doubt shape the pastoral care extended toward the persons involved, but, Bonhoeffer insisted, such circumstances "cannot in any way alter the fact of murder."[98]

Given Bonhoeffer's intense conception of the church's responsibility for the world and his eventual participation in the conspiracy to assassinate Hitler, largely driven by his growing awareness of the atrocities being committed by the Nazi regime, it is difficult to imagine that Bonhoeffer would advise silence in the face of abortion on demand. Indeed, it would seem more natural to expect that Bonhoeffer would share the identification of abortion on demand as an ongoing holocaust compelling protest by the church. And yet, interest in this anti-abortion stance among Bonhoeffer scholars has been muted at best and is completely lacking at worst.

Chapter Five

FREEDOM, SUFFERING, AND HOPE

Seek God, not happiness.[99]

DIETRICH BONHOEFFER, *LIFE TOGETHER*

Happiness is the promise of Heaven . . . holiness is the priority here in this world.[100]

DAVID DOCKERY

The Blood of the Martyrs is the Seed of the Church.[101]

TERTULLIAN

DURING THE LAST YEARS of his life, Karl Barth rarely preached a sermon except to prisoners. The word circulated that if you wanted to hear Barth preach you had first to commit a felony! Barth once commented that he enjoyed preaching to prisoners because they needed no help in appreciating the fact of their bondage and the longing for freedom and that this is the subject the gospel. Bonhoeffer, like his teacher, received the good news of Jesus Christ as an offer of freedom, indeed as a call to freedom.

Following the failed attempt upon Hitler's life on July 20, 1944, Bonhoeffer lost hope of release from prison and fully expected that, sooner or later, he would he executed. On July 21, on the heels of the reception of this devastating realization, he composed the poem "Stages on the Road to Freedom." There he delineated four stages or dimensions characteristic of the enjoyment of Christian freedom: (1) discipline, (2) action, (3) suffering, and (4) death. One might also understand these stages as dimensions of Christian freedom since, strictly speaking, enjoyment of freedom is possible along the way:

Stages on the Road to Freedom

Discipline

If you set out to seek freedom, then learn above all things to govern your soul and your senses, for fear that your passions and longing may lead you away from the path you should follow. Only through discipline may a man learn to be free.

Action

Daring to do what is right, not what fancy may tell you,
Valiantly grasping occasions, not cravenly doubting—

Freedom comes only through deeds, not through thoughts taking wing.
Faint not nor fear, but go out to the storm and the action, trusting in God whose commandment you faithfully follow; freedom, exultant, will welcome your spirit with joy.

Suffering

A change has come indeed. Your hands, so strong and active, are bound; in helplessness now you see your action is ended; you sigh in relief, your cause committing to stronger hands; so now you may rest contented. Only for one blissful moment could you draw near to touch freedom; then, that it might be perfected in glory, you gave it to God.

Death

Come now, thou greatest of feasts on the journey to freedom eternal; death, cast aside all the burdensome chains, and demolish the walls of our temporal body, the walls of our souls that are blinded, so that at last we see that which here remains hidden.
Freedom, how long we have sought thee in discipline, action, and suffering; dying, we may behold thee revealed in the Lord.[102]

This poem, composed at the end of Bonhoeffer's short life, demonstrates a certain continuity of conviction stretching back at least to the writing of *Cost of Discipleship*, namely, impatience with passivity, resignation, or nonchalance regarding the world Jesus died to save. Once the pressure and possibility of self-justification are excluded once and for all by the cross, one crucial and spectacular aspect of Christian freedom emerges—freedom to act! Coming into the tempest of living becomes possible for those who live under the forgiveness offered in Jesus Christ. And the prize includes especially identification and true communion with Jesus.

Happiness

Perhaps no quote from the Bonhoeffer corpus contrasts more obviously with the Western spirituality of the twenty-first century than the one heading this chapter. Perhaps it is true that where Christians are not persecuted, where the church makes peace with culture, Christianity becomes one more competing strategy for personal happiness. "Happiness"—an enduringly enticing yet stubbornly elusive concept—and yet all that suggests itself to the human heart at the mention of this word takes center stage in God's revelation in the Bible. Here we are led to sing of peace, take refuge in God, and exult in worship. Here we are commanded, "Be not anxious," "Do not fret." Instead, "Rejoice," indeed, "Rejoice always and again I say rejoice!" In the Sermon on the Mount, Jesus begins with happiness. The promise given for the sustaining and encouragement of the persecuted church must inflame the yearning of all who have suffered the blows and devastations of earthly existence. "He will wipe away every tear from their eyes. Death will exist no longer; grief, crying, and pain will exist no longer, because the previous things have passed away" (Rev. 21:4).

Bonhoeffer certainly sought and enjoyed not a little happiness during his short time on this earth. He exhibited no signs of the martyr complex one might expect of one caught up in the struggles and oppositions that characterized his life. His behavior could not have contrasted more from any sort of morbid or masochistic fixation with suffering. Just the opposite. While he did often convey a definite seriousness of purpose, friends and acquaintances alike encountered in him a radiant enthusiasm and hope, even in prison, as this remembrance from 1945 makes clear: "Bonhoeffer always seemed to me to spread an atmosphere of happiness and joy over the least incident and profound gratitude for the mere fact that he was alive."[103]

Yet Bonhoeffer did identify the *pursuit* of happiness as a distinctive enemy of Christian discipleship. He expected meditation on the Word of God to provoke all manner of darkness and struggle within the soul of believers. This darkness and emptiness exposes our selfishness and sinfulness and should prompt confession and repentance. Immature believers avoid such confrontation with the truth about themselves and so also forfeit the natural pattern of true discipleship which necessarily involves being sunk low in order that one might be raised up by the merciful and forgiving Spirit of God.

Meditation on the Word teaches the disciple to seek and expect everything good from God in his own Word, notwithstanding the agony of facing the truth of one's sinfulness again and again: "We must center our attention on the Word alone and leave consequences to its action. For may it not be that God Himself sends us these hours of reproof and dryness that we may be brought again to expect everything from His Word? 'Seek God, not happiness'—this the fundamental rule of all meditation. It you seek God alone, you will gain happiness: that is its promise."[104]

Bonhoeffer preached boldly to others of the self-denial Jesus called for. And when the moment came for decision, Bonhoeffer walked the walk. The authenticity of the man's early convictions is proved in the later decisions. He deserves the status of martyr because he knowingly risked his life for the sake of obedience to his Lord, and that obedience stands as witness to the lordship and glory of God in the face of Jesus Christ.

Freedom from Self

Bonhoeffer's attraction to the active life can be viewed against the backdrop of the keen sense of his own sinful heart. As a student of seventeen, before a hushed classroom, Bonhoeffer, for the first time, announced his long-held intention to become a theologian. This unplanned self-exposure led to tortuous introspection in which he examined his conflicting feelings about the incident. What he found, among other things, were vanity and pride. Bonhoeffer never forgot the discovery of the hollowness and selfish ambition of his early devotedness and religiosity. Competitive by nature, he nevertheless recognized the utter incompatibility of this instinct, at least in the spiritual realm, and also, importantly, with Christian freedom.

From early on, a good Lutheran I suppose, Bonhoeffer understood the self-deception which too often sustains the dream of personal progress in holiness. Living under grace, exposing oneself to the judgment of God, clinging to the cross, taking comfort in the alien righteousness of Christ—these belonged to the disciple's walk with God, not self-congratulation, not the tracking of one's supposed daily incremental closing of the gap between Christ's holiness and one's own.

Meditation on the Word of God was just that, meditation of the Word, not on oneself as such. Confession, repentance, worship, and service were its proper fruits, not personal fulfillment or personal enrichment per se. Since, for Bonhoeffer, the believer has all things in Christ, to turn one's eyes from him to oneself promised only disappointment, spiritual impotence, and defeat. Christian obedience could not and so should presume to secure what is already achieved for us and available to us only in Christ. Obedience lives from faith in the finished work of Christ on our behalf and so reflects the truth of forgiveness, mercy, and hope declared in him. Obedience lives from these things; it does not achieve them.

Freedom to Obey

The politically correct orthodoxy of our day would confine religious belief to the private sphere. It would be difficult to imagine a notion more alien to Bonhoeffer's thinking. For Bonhoeffer the truth revealed in Jesus Christ lays upon believers a distinct responsibility for the world claimed by its Ceator, Sustainer, and Judge. We who recognize in the cross and resurrection the revelation of God are called to bear witness to his will not only or even especially for our individual lives but for the church and the world. True discipleship, for Bonhoeffer, compels the articulation of religiously informed belief in the public square. Failure to do so would constitute the hiding of one's light under a bushel.

Freedom from Self-Justification

"We cannot ourselves examine whether our hearing [of the Word of God] and our doing are true or false; indeed this will depend precisely on whether or not we entrust this examination entirely to the knowledge and judgment of Jesus."[105] Salvation by grace through faith, while perhaps leaving a place for self-examination, nevertheless excludes claims to have God on one's side in this or that action. Only appeal to Scripture is allowed, and in such a case one remains under the Scripture, exposed to its judgment. One cannot rise above the Bible, becoming its judge.

The slightest lapse into self-justifying claims for the righteousness of one's activity immediately compromises the goodness of the action in question because it has abandoned the walk of faith for the walk of sight. One has ceased to be a doer of the law in favor of presuming to judge the law. To walk by faith means to walk in dependence upon God's mercy and forgiveness. Internal incentive to act so as to please God does not diminish but is heightened or perhaps better, takes on the indispensable character of genuinely righteous behavior, namely, that it has lost all need for self-justification which inevitably supposes to lay some claim upon God and nurture interest in comparison with one's brother.

For Bonhoeffer the Christian is free for the impossibility and thus also the burden of self-justification. As such, believers are free to do their best, with God's help, to hear and obey the command of God in Holy Scripture, leaving the judging where it belongs, with God revealed in Jesus Christ. Such faith-shaped freedom for action corresponds both to utter dependence upon God and to forgiveness-shaped love for fellow believers.

This Christian freedom—what Luther cryptically called "sinning boldly and letting grace abound"—has nothing to do with indifference to God's law or the concreteness of God's commands. Bonhoeffer is not retreating from the notion of absolute truth, nor does he shy away from the question, "Is this or that action more in keeping with God's revealed will?" What is rejected is self-justification because of its impossibility and its irrelevance in light of the cross of Jesus Christ. What Bonhoeffer means to preserve is the disciple's walk of faith and the special freedom for obedience purchased for believers in the death of Jesus.

Note Bonhoeffer's reading of Matthew 7:21–23 wherein the Lord dispatches claimants to righteous living with blunt dismissal: "I never knew you! Depart from Me, you lawbreakers!" Bonhoeffer accounts for Jesus' rejection of their profession of allegiance to Christ "because they arise from the man's own knowledge of good and evil."[106]

Bonhoeffer expected that believers would do everything in their power to identify the action required by God of his people in their own time and place. They would plunge into the difficulties and joys and sufferings of the world. They would pray. And especially they would study and meditate upon God's Word in Holy Scripture. But ultimately they would not presume to judge their own actions. They would leave that to the only true Judge. They would do their best and offer their efforts to the heavenly Father for his judgment, thus living by forgiveness, mercy, and grace.

Freedom, Not Choice

For all Bonhoeffer's "falling short" before evangelical eyes, his departure from the reigning liberalism of his day was certainly profound. Like Barth, Bonhoeffer's recognition of the sovereignty of God fell comfortably within the Augustinian-Lutheran tradition. Accordingly, when Bonhoeffer speaks of freedom, he never has in mind a kind of Pelagian or even Arminian notion of choice-making power. The state of unbelievers vis-à-vis God is best characterized as bondage, not freedom. Freedom must be bestowed upon sinners, and its exercise always means obedience to God's Word, never disobedience or a choice between the two. Disobedience is an exercise of bondage. Obedience is an exercise of freedom.

Command as Permission

Bonhoeffer also rejected early on the false dichotomy between freedom and command, between law and grace. The Ten Commandments of the Decalogue of Exodus is preceded by the recalling of Israel's deliverance from Egyptian bondage for a reason. Likewise the Sermon on the Mount begins with the Beatitudes. God's command is, first of all, God's permission. God's commands are gracious invitations to share the life of God through participation in God's shaping of the future. Thus Bonhoeffer found gospel in the Old Testament as well as the New. Commenting on the Psalms he writes:

> It is grace to know God's commands. They release us from self-made plans and conflicts. They make our steps certain and our way joyful. God gives his commands in order that we may fulfill them, and "his commandments are not burdensome" (1 John 5:3) for him who has found all salvation in Jesus Christ. Jesus has himself been under the law and has fulfilled it in total obedience to the Father. God's will becomes his joy, his nourishment. So he gives thanks in us for the grace of the law and grants to us joy in its fulfillment. Now we confess our love for the law, we affirm that we gladly keep it, and we ask that we may continue to be kept blameless in it. We do that not in our own power, but we pray it in the name of Jesus Christ who is for us and in us.[107]

Bonhoeffer read Luther's "sin boldly and let grace abound" as a Word of liberation from the paralyzing and finally unnecessary burden of claiming God's direct sanction for actions taken in obedience to the Word of God. Bonhoeffer quoted 2 Chronicles 20:12 more often than any other passage: "We do not know what to do, but we look to You." We live by grace, by the forgiveness of sins even, no, especially, as disciples obeying their Lord.

Suffering and Hope

Sixty years after his death, Bonhoeffer's ethical and theological writings continue to attract scholarly and popular attention. Use of Bonhoeffer has come conspicuously and disproportionately from liberal and progressive ranks. There are good reasons for a certain evangelical wariness regarding Bonhoeffer. Still, profound departures from progressivist methodology and ideology in Bonhoeffer's writings remain undeniable and certainly were not lost on contemporaries to his left. What we might call the "simple biblicist" strain in Bonhoeffer's thought and practice was found particularly galling and worrisome by many. His unashamed embrace of the heart work appropriate to discipleship together with a definite quest for Spirit-empowered obedience suggested a lapse into emotionalism to others. Now, as we consider Bonhoeffer's understanding of freedom and hope, once again we encounter a voice closer to evangelical orthodoxy than to anything progressive.

Bonhoeffer believed in divine sovereignty and divine providence. And Bonhoeffer believed in heaven. Yes, he did indicate awareness of a resignation and passivity inducing danger where a distortive and unbiblical preoccupation with heaven prevails. But for all Bonhoeffer's emphasis on the responsibility of the Christian believer and the church for the future, he was clear in his conviction that, ultimately and thus concretely, the future lies in the hands of God, not of men. Liberal and progressive readings of Bonhoeffer often neglect such emphases within the Bonhoeffer corpus, but their presence is unmistakable and striking. Liberals and progressives often reject outright or take refuge in mystery or agnosticism on the question of God's sovereignty and providence. One explanation for such squeamishness in the face of prominent biblical teaching is, no doubt, a certain protectiveness of human responsibility. Fear of weakening the incentives they find necessary for obedience, moral striving, and responsibility prevents uninhibited embrace of the afterlife and the permanent deliverance from this fallen world it promises.

Bonhoeffer recognized the biblical relationship between obedience and heaven, between promise and persecution. Disciples of Jesus Christ bear up under persecution and suffering not only or even principally out of gratitude for the forgiveness of sins achieved on the cross. Rather, the promise of heaven sustains them. God's promise to raise them from the dead unto new and eternal life in paradise stiffens the witness's resolve in the face of opposition and even the prospect of death.

Bonhoeffer reserved a tiny chapter of less than four pages in his *Cost of Discipleship* to comment on Matthew 10:26–39. A few extended excerpts from this chapter entitled "Decision" should make clear the crucial connection between the promise of heaven and the duty of disciples, messengers of the Word, in Bonhoeffer's thinking. This first excerpt validates and encourages the disciple's desire that his witness for Christ not be in vain and promises public vindication of the faithful messenger of the Word.

> The messengers abide by the Word, and the Word abides by the messengers, now and in all eternity. Three times Jesus encourages his disciples by saying, "Fear not." Although their sufferings are now secret, they will not always be so; some day they will be made manifest before God and man. However secret these sufferings are at present, they have their Lord's promise that they will be eventually brought to the light of day. And that will mean glory for the messengers and judgment for their persecutors.[108]

The appropriateness and appeal of the Lord's "do not fear" is grounded not merely in the promise to vindicate the message delivered but the messenger too:

> They must not fear men. Men can do them no harm, for the power of men ceases with the death of the body. But

they must overcome the fear of death with the fear of God. The danger lies not in the judgment of God, not in the death of the body but in the eternal destruction of body and soul. Those who are still afraid of men have no fear of God, and those who have fear of God have ceased to be afraid of men. All preachers of the gospel will do well to recollect this saying daily.[109]

Do not these words strike us as wholly appropriate for conservative, Bible-believing, evangelical ears and yet also somehow unwelcome among us these days? Missionary mandate. Self-denial. Courage. Heaven. Hell. Judgment! Yes, Bonhoeffer has something to say that we evangelicals need to hear—an insistence that the words of Jesus be received as the Word of God for our lives now, today!

The Lord calls his disciples not to resignation, not to defeatism, but to faith and hope in the faithful God who keeps his promises. Our God is the providential ruler of the universe. His enemies never stray beyond the bounds circumscribed by him. Nor can his enemies ultimately threaten his good plans for his messengers on earth:

The power which men enjoy for a brief space on earth is not without the cognizance and the will of God. If we fall into the hands of men, and meet suffering and death from their violence, we are none the less certain that everything comes from God. The same God who sees no sparrow fall to the ground without his knowledge and will, allows nothing to happen, except it be good and profitable for his children and the cause for which they stand. We are in God's hands. Therefore, "Fear not."[110]

Heaven and Earth

Bonhoeffer found the promise of heaven and the return of Jesus Christ riveting. Friends and acquaintances alike were, in the words of his closest friend, "astonished at its immediacy to him and the fervor of his attitude to it."[111] Notably, Bonhoeffer's zeal for the return of Jesus had special meaning for him in the area of pastoral ministry and particularly in the catechizing of children.

Christians of all ages, particularly those who have suffered, and even more particularly those who have suffered for their faith, have clung to the divine promise of paradise beyond this vale of tears. Such enduring belief in the next world can be traced directly to the revelation of God in Holy Scripture. Christian hope for heaven is no projection of human need but the appropriate response to the promise of Almighty God. Dismissal of the doctrine of heaven as pie-in-the-sky religion by self-declared Christians involves a contradiction in terms. Belief in heaven is no optional doctrine designed for the weak. God declares what he intends to accomplish. The God who reveals his plans for his twice-born children also insists that they believe, embrace, and celebrate the truth of this promise. Belief in the resurrection of the dead to eternal life in paradise is a constituent dimension of the Christian life. God has promised these things, and to suppose otherwise displays not only ingratitude but falsehood. To live without the promise of heaven is to live according to a lie.

It is certainly true that Christians have found ways to misuse and abuse the clear teaching of God on many matters, and the doctrine of heaven is no exception. Wherever a distorted, disproportional, and isolated fixation on the afterlife results in apathy, escapism, and retreat from the duties of this earthly life, biblical Christianity has been abandoned, and fleshly desire has gained control. Bonhoeffer understood this, and his response contrasts sharply with liberals and progressives so prone to throw the baby out with the bathwater.

Unbiblical construals of the doctrine of heaven sometimes result in Christians so heavenly minded as to be of little earthly use. The Confessing Church itself had exhibited real tension at this point as Hitler's reign of terror proceeded. One group, with which Bonhoeffer identified, insisted that the church had ethical and prophetic obligations in the face of the Nazi menace while others turned more and more inward, concentrating exclusively on the nurture of its own spiritual life. This latter group often combined a sharp apocalyptic strain with its resignation in the face of Hitler's terror. But, like the heroes of Hebrews' roll call of faith (Heb. 11–12), Bonhoeffer knew that God's promise of heaven is meant to (and in actual fact it does) sustain responsible engagement with the demands of this life. The heroes of Hebrews 11–12 were so heavenly minded so as to be of the greatest possible earthly use: they all "died in faith without having received the promises" (Heb. 11:13). They acknowledged that they were "foreigners and temporary residents on the earth" (Heb. 11:13). They desired "a better land—a heavenly one" (Heb. 11:16). And note God's own interest in this desire among those who have faith—"Therefore God is not ashamed to be called their God, for he has prepared a city for them" (Heb. 11:26).

The faith spoken of in Hebrews 11–12 focuses both on Jesus as the pioneer of faith and upon that "city that has foundations, whose architect and builder is God" toward which Jesus' followers inevitably move (Heb. 11:10). In what does this faith result? By faith "they crossed the Red Sea as if they were on dry ground," "the walls of Jericho fell down," "Rahab the prostitute did not perish" (Heb. 11:30–31). By faith they:

> conquered kingdoms, administered justice, obtained prom-
> ises, shut the mouths of lions, quenched the raging of fire,
> escaped the edge of the sword, gained strength after being
> weak, became mighty in battle, and put foreign armies to
> flight. Women received their dead raised to life again. Some
> men were tortured, not accepting release, so that they might
> gain a better resurrection, and others experienced mock-
> ings, and scourgings, as well as bonds and imprisonment.
> They were stoned, they were sawed in two, they died by the
> sword, they wandered about in sheepskins, in goatskins, des-
> titute, afflicted, and mistreated. The world was not worthy
> of them. (Heb. 11:33–38)

The writer of Hebrews sets forth models of faith: a following faith, an
obedient faith, an active faith, and, especially, a faith willing and able
to act responsibly in and for this world with and because of its keen eye
toward heaven. Hankering after the next world may produce apathy,
resignation, and retreat from the duties of this life, but it should not
and it need not. Belief in the afterlife may just as well render sacrificial
love, courageous obedience, and bold proclamation of the gospel rea-
sonable where the temptation to rationalize one's cowardice and sell
out to the world might otherwise prevail. In the great models of faith
in Hebrews, we are confronted with believers so heavenly minded that
they become of the greatest possible earthly use.

Whether heaven and hell lie beyond the grave irrevocably alters
the cost benefit analysis confronting would-be followers of the crucified Jesus. What did the apostle Paul say? "If we have placed our hope
in Christ for this life only, we should be pitied more than anyone." And
furthermore, accepting the validity of a first-century pagan philosophy
of life should there be no life beyond this world, "If the dead are not
raised, Let us eat and drink, for tomorrow we die" (1 Cor. 15:19, 32).

Certainly, whether heaven awaits followers of Jesus Christ has nothing to do with how belief in the fact affects this or that person or community of faith. But where Christians suffer, embrace of divine promises of resurrection and eternal life tends to follow. Bonhoeffer noticed the prominence of heaven in the preaching and singing among African-American Christians during his time in New York City. There he saw firsthand that yearning for heaven might sustain faith and love in the midst of suffering. What Bonhoeffer grew to despise was any weakening of the inextricable link between discipleship and suffering. Where he drew back from fixation on the next world, he typically did so out of protectiveness for the necessity of suffering as Christians in this world.

As for the heroes of Hebrews, so for Bonhoeffer, belief in the afterlife and responsibility in this life are not enemies but friends. To pit the two teachings against each other is to misunderstand both:

> There are people who regard it as frivolous, and some Christians think it impious, for anyone to hope and prepare for a better earthly future. They think that the meaning of present events is chaos, disorder and catastrophe; and in resignation or pious escapism they surrender all responsibility for reconstruction and for future generations. It may be that the day of judgment will dawn tomorrow; in that case, we shall gladly stop working for a better future. But not before.[112]

Bonhoeffer believed in the imminent return of Jesus and related this conviction directly to the urgency to call unbelievers to repentance.[113] To withhold or even delay the call to repentance displayed an acute lack of charity toward one's fellowman who could face Christ as judge at any moment. The lordship of Christ over the world was an established fact for Bonhoeffer, and the imminent return of Christ only heightened the urgency for Christ's followers to become living witnesses to the reality of that lordship.

In *The Cost of Discipleship* Bonhoeffer emphasized the exclusivity of Christ's lordship; only he is Lord. In the later unfinished *Ethics* the universal scope of Christ's lordship took center stage; Christ is Lord of all things, including especially this present world. Christ's return, his second coming, involves the universal revelation of Christ as the one he has always been—Lord of all. Christ's disciples have the privilege of knowing Christ as Lord before the universal revelation of that fact befalls the whole creation and have the happy duty to announce his coming and to bear witness to him in both word and deed. Yes, Bonhoeffer recognized the danger of treating the promise of heaven as a refuge and escape from responsibility in this world. But he recognized that in Scripture and in the biblically shaped faith of the disciples, eschatology and ethics went hand in hand because the Lord of heaven is also the Lord of this earth.

In his *Letters and Papers from Prison* it seems clear that Bonhoeffer saw how the biblical teaching on heaven could and should serve to undergird Christian responsibility for this world, "The Christian hope of resurrection . . . sends human beings back to their lives on earth in a wholly new way."[114]

We do find tension in Bonhoeffer's treatment of the doctrine of heaven, and not a creative tension in my view but an unresolved conflict solvable by his better insights reviewed above. Nevertheless Bonhoeffer's reasons for hesitance are, in a certain way, praiseworthy, especially given his own self-conscious willingness to die if obedience to Christ required it. As we have seen, Bonhoeffer's wariness concerning the afterlife arose not as a matter of principle or of confusion regarding the clear teaching of the Bible but from his awareness of the wrong use to which the doctrine was often put.

Both in his thinking and his living, Bonhoeffer probably abhorred nothing so much as resignation, apathy, and passivity in regard to this world. Consequently, we find Bonhoeffer keenly protective of the Christian necessity of obedience, responsibility, risk-taking, and self-forgetful, self-denying sacrifice for others. He did not see himself as a giant in these things by any means, but he did accept them as concrete requirements of his crucified and risen Savior and Lord. And when we remember Bonhoeffer's reading of the crucial and fearful role that suffering must play in the redeeming work of Christ, we begin to understand his sometimes tentative, sometimes contradictory statements about the promise of eternal life.

Another Lutheran, Søren Kierkegaard (1813–55), identified within his own church a century earlier in Denmark this same danger and distortion. Kierkegaard's remarkable treatment of Abraham's divinely commanded, then aborted, sacrifice of Isaac in *Fear and Trembling* (1843) crystallizes certain concerns Bonhoeffer would come to share. Rembrandt's "Sacrifice of Isaac" depicts Abraham's raised knife-wielding hand, poised for the plunge into the chest of Isaac, the son of promise, born to parents "as good as dead!" (Heb. 11:11, 19). But alas, already the angel's hand descends to restrain Abraham's, and the ram, the sacrifice provided by the Lord, is already there, entangled in the thicket, ready to take Isaac's place on the makeshift altar. For Kierkegaard the joyous deliverance comes too soon. Whoever would understand Abraham and so also understand the character of Christian faith must back up and slow down. Rembrandt, so like ourselves, rushes to the resolution, not lingering to muse on what had to precede the intervention of the angel and the appearance of the ram. And so Kierkegaard obliges the reader to pause, to contemplate Abraham's cleaving of the wood, his sharpening of the knife, and the three days' journey with the mountain of sacrifice looming in the distance as father and son moved ever so deliberately toward the horror of God's command (Gen. 22).[115]

Bonhoeffer, like Kierkegaard, would bid us pause and let the true character of faith sink in. Saving faith exhibits trust in God through suffering born of obedience. Deliverance is promised and hoped for but not snatched at. The suffering, the trouble Jesus foretold concerning his disciples comes first, and then the joy (John 16:33). Those who fail to grasp this fail to understand both the call of Jesus and the meaning of the incarnation. And they forfeit the special happiness of the obedient disciple. A happiness enjoyed proleptically, as it were, through Spirit-empowered faith in the promise spoken by God the Son, the suffering servant:

> I assure you: you will weep and wail, but the world
> will rejoice. You will become sorrowful, but your sorrow
> will turn to joy. When a woman is in labor she has pain
> because her time has come. But when she has given birth
> to a child, she no longer remembers the suffering because
> of the joy that a person has been born into the world. So
> you also have sorrow now. But I will see you again. Your
> hearts will rejoice, and no one will rob you of your joy.
> (John 16:20–22)

Reception of the divine promise is not the same as full and permanent possession of that deliverance. But neither is reception of the promise the same as not having the deliverance at all. When husband and wife are made prospective parents by the news that the woman is pregnant, preparation for the promised child commences at once. No one can know if the child will come to term or if either mother or baby will survive the birth process. But, no matter, they have the promise, and so experience of joy for the hoped-for baby becomes not only possible at once but really compulsory. Unlike this common experience referenced by Jesus as he prepared his disciples for his bodily departure and their own impending suffering, God fulfills his promises perfectly every time. The promise of a child might fail, but God's promised deliverance is certain. How much more then ought that promise to kindle joy in the hearts and minds of believing disciples when the suffering foretold falls upon them?

Bonhoeffer, his caveats regarding the doctrine of heaven notwithstanding, understood these connections between heaven, obedience, promise-sustained endurance of suffering, and promise-produced joy:

> Joy belongs, not only to those who have been called home,
> but also to the living, and no one shall take it from us. We
> are one with them in this joy, but never in sorrow. . . .
> I don't mean by this something fabricated, compelled, but
> something given, free. Joy dwells with God; it descends
> from him and seizes spirit, soul, and body, and where this
> joy has grasped a man it grows greater, carries him away,
> opens closed doors. . . . The joy of God has been through
> the poverty of the crib and the distress of the cross; there-
> fore it is insuperable, irrefutable. It does not deny the dis-
> tress where it is, but finds God in the midst of it, indeed
> precisely there; it does not contest the most grievous sin, but
> finds forgiveness in just this way; it looks death in the face,
> yet finds life in death itself.[116]

God does not produce endurance in his servants by lying to them about evil or suffering. Escapist resignation and passive irresponsibility have no place in biblical Christianity. Neither does any glib, dismissive, smiley-face response to the suffering of others. But equally false is any construal of reality or its meaning apart from the saving work of God in Christ or the promise of final redemption, deliverance from this world, the elimination of pain, the wiping away of tears, the death of death, and yes, eternal bliss. Because to do so is itself a lie. God does not call suffering *not suffering,* and neither should we. But he does set beside the stark and brutal reality of evil and suffering another reality equally true: God is up to the suffering and evil, including the debt of our sins, and has exposed himself to all of this for our sakes, and has triumphed! You who were dead in trespasses and sins, God made alive together with Christ and your life is hidden with him (Eph. 2:1; Col. 3:13–14; Rom. 8:18).

Putting at risk one's own earthly happiness, abandoning treasured comforts, forsaking oneself for the sake of Christ and others are at the heart of Christian discipleship. This is the teaching of God's Word, the example of God's own Son, and the revealed expectation for God's children, "and if children, also heirs—heirs of God and co-heirs with Christ—seeing that we suffer with Him so that we may also be glorified with Him" (Rom. 8:17).

Pilgrims and Strangers

Keenly aware of the dangers of an escapist fixation on the promise of heaven, Bonhoeffer's references to this subject grew increasingly spare and muted. He did not bring the same reticence in preaching, especially when emphasizing the role of suffering in the life of disciples of Jesus:

> I am a sojourner on earth. But I recognize that I cannot abide here, that my time is short. Nor do I have rights here to possessions or a home. I must receive with gratitude all the good that befalls me, but I must suffer injustice and violence without anyone interceding for me.

Because I am nothing but a sojourner on earth, with no rights, no support and no security; because God himself has made me so weak and insignificant, he has given me one firm pledge of my goal: his Word. He will not take this one security from me; he will keep this Word with me, and by it he will allow me to feel my strength.

The life of the Christian community in the world bears permanent witness to the truth that "the fashion of this world is passing away," that the time is short, and the Lord is nigh. This thought fills them with Joy unspeakable.[117]

The world is growing too small for the Christian community, and all it looks for is the Lord's return. It still walks in the flesh, but with eyes upturned to heaven, whence he for whom they wait will come again.

In the world the Christians are a colony of the true home, they are strangers and aliens in a foreign land, enjoying the hospitality of that land, obeying its laws and honoring its government. They receive with gratitude the requirements of their bodily life, and in all things prove themselves honest, just, chaste, gentle, peaceable, and ready to serve. They are patient and cheerful in suffering, and they glory in tribulation.

But they are only passing through the country. At any moment they may receive the signal to move on. Then they will strike tents, leaving behind them all their worldly friends and connections, and following only the voice of their Lord who calls. They leave the land of their exile, and start their homeward trek to heaven.[118]

Evangelicals and Middle-Class Values

In Bonhoeffer do we not recognize a disturbingly rare embrace of passages such as this one from 2 Timothy: "But know this; difficult times will come in the last days. For people will be lovers of self, lovers of money, boastful, proud, blasphemers, disobedient to parents, ungrateful, unholy, unloving, irreconcilable, slanderers, without self-control, brutal, without love for what is good, traitors, reckless, conceited, lovers of pleasure rather than lovers of God, holding to the form of religion but denying its power" (3:1–5).

Surely part of the American evangelical attraction to Christianized self-help and personal success-fixated literature arises from a natural, predictable tension afflicting the evangelical psyche—the tension between intended submission to an authoritative Bible and immersion in the materialistic culture of the wealthiest nation in history. In such an atmosphere much of Scripture seems irrelevant to our lives. Perhaps two-thirds or more of the New Testament targets an audience faced with immediate threat of persecution for their faith. By persecution the New Testament authors have in mind not mild ostracism—say not being invited to the annual neighborhood beer bash—but threats to livelihood and life itself. Yet we evangelicals are the Bible people, people of the book. The pressure to make something of the texts before us becomes acute. Too often the result has been to press the Scriptures into the service of middle-class values inimical to the gospel of Jesus Christ.

Surely one explanation for Bonhoeffer's continued attraction is simply the authenticity of his faith. Christians who are immersed in this wealth-and-success-focused culture but also read their Bibles detect the mark of authenticity in Bonhoeffer, and the Spirit of God within us craves such identification with our crucified Savior. Is it not true that something in us is perhaps not satisfied exactly by acquaintance with Bonhoeffer's story but is stimulated by it in a unique way? In Bonhoeffer we allow ourselves to be told something not dissimilar to the words of Jesus to the rich young ruler, "leave everything." We recognize that when Bonhoeffer abandoned the teaching post in New York City and returned to Germany and possible death, he was obeying the same Christ who died for us and whom we love. We realize with perhaps a mixture of joy and sadness that Bonhoeffer gave our Lord something he asks from us too but has not received. Are we not glad in a special way that, if we are not following Jesus as he deserves, that somebody, somewhere did?

Does not Bonhoeffer's question convict us? "What are we really devoted to? That is the question. Are our hearts set on earthly goods? Do we try to combine loyalty to them with devotion to Christ? Or are we devoted exclusively to Him?"[119] Ought we not lift up the "Bonhoeffers" among us, rare though they be, rather than others too entangled with the values of the world? Does not Bonhoeffer appear to us at once strange and familiar—strange in so far as we cling to self and security, familiar in so far as we read our Bibles, give ourselves to others for Christ's sake, and yield to the prompting of the Holy Spirit?

The rise of the Third Reich, because it targeted the church as a likely enemy, set the stage for the exposure of what we might call true New Testament Christianity. What I mean is that church leaders and Christians generally found themselves confronted with a decision closely matching the one so common to first-century believers, namely, stand up for Christ or expose yourself and your family to the worst horrors of persecution.

Christ's Suffering and Ours

Perhaps Bonhoeffer's most significant adoption of Barth's dogmatism appears in his doctrine of Christ. God reveals himself to us in Jesus Christ, the incarnate one. God will be known there or known wrongly, that is, not known at all. Revelation alone offers the hope of true acquaintance with the holy Creator and Redeemer of the world. Nothing in the created order, least of all within the fallen nature of man, provides a means to the true knowledge of God. Only free, divine self-disclosure promises genuine comprehension of God.

But, alas, just this has happened. The only true God, the Creator of the universe, the Judge of living and dead, for his own purposes, chiefly to glorify himself, has in fact given himself to be known by hell-deserving sinners like you and me. He has revealed himself in and as Jesus Christ. God confronts us in Jesus Christ not merely as the means to true and saving knowledge of God, but as God himself, divine and human from and unto all eternity. In Jesus Christ we meet not merely the means to salvation but the Savior himself.

Classic Christian confession insists that, in Jesus Christ, God became man without ceasing to be God. And so he did. But this means that any notion that divinity might be threatened by taking on humanity was always wrong. Since God reveals himself as Jesus Christ, we know that true deity includes true humanity not only without ceasing to be divine but as an ordinary expression of true deity. Deity and humanity may be distinguished but not separated. If man finds himself alienated from the life of God, this can only highlight the distorted, false, judged, and damned humanity with which he has to do. True humanity is embodied in Jesus Christ alone.

Bonhoeffer's concept of Christ existing as community is striking, and we can certainly recognize the exegetical sources for such a notion. The "in Christ" and "body" language of the Pauline corpus have long resulted in interpretations similar to Bonhoeffer's. However, such language has been read by some to suggest a kind of radical identification, or even reduction, of Christ with the community of believers. Such is not the case with Bonhoeffer.

Bonhoeffer's teacher Karl Barth, though Swiss reformed and thus predisposed to wariness toward images of Jesus Christ, nevertheless insisted upon having Matthias Grünewald's famous painting *The Crucifixion* before him as he wrote his massive *Church Dogmatics*. In this painting Jesus hangs from the cross as Mary, John, and Mary Magdalene stand by on one side while on the other side stands John the Baptist. The Baptist, with one hand, holds the Scriptures open to the place where it is written, "He must increase, but I must decrease," as, with the other hand, he points with an elongated, prophetic finger at the crucified Jesus (John 3:30). Barth saw in this painting an apt depiction of the role of the church in the world—to point away from itself to the Savior of the world, the only one who ultimately can deliver from sin, death, hell, and the devil. The church functions, in speech and life, as witness to him who can save.

That Bonhoeffer shared this view is unmistakable and also crucial so as to avoid any notion of the community of believers as a replacement for Christ. Distinction between the believer, the church, and Christ becomes especially significant in relation to suffering: "Some of us suffer a great deal from having our senses dulled in the face of all the sorrows which these wars have brought with them. And yet we must be careful not to confuse ourselves with Christ. . . . Christ endured all suffering and all human guilt to the full. But Christ could suffer alongside men because at the same time he was able to redeem them from suffering."[120]

Perseverance in service and ministry within the community of faith and to the world depended in some measure upon a clear demarcation between the role of the church and the role of the Savior himself. Where this distinction is lost, believers may futilely attempt to take upon themselves burdens only Christ can bear. No favor is done when the church points to itself rather than to its Lord as the Redeemer and unnecessary exhaustion and despair threaten where the church turns inward for its resources. By God's good pleasure and original purpose in creation, believers are permanently set within into dependency upon God; and their witness to the world points them too, away from themselves and toward their God. It is still true that, as we have seen, believers are set within a mutually dependent relationship upon one another within the body of Christ, which is the church; but as that body they live from their head who is Christ!

One consequence of this reality is the qualification and limitation of the burden borne by the church in this fallen world:

> We are not called to burden ourselves with the sorrows of the whole world; in the end, we cannot suffer with men in our own strength because we are unable to redeem. A suppressed desire to suffer with man in one's own strength must come to resignation. We simply look with utter joy on the one who really suffered with men and became their Redeemer. . . . Only in such joy towards Christ, the redeemer, are we saved from having our senses dulled by the pressure of human sorrow, or from becoming resigned under the experiences of suffering.[121]

Suffering never becomes, for Bonhoeffer, a thing good in itself. Suffering remains suffering. Jesus does not laugh upon hearing of Lazarus's death; he weeps. Jesus does not strut toward the cross; he begs his heavenly father to let the cup pass from him. No, Bonhoeffer does not paste a smiley face on human suffering, but he does recognize in Christ the limits within which evil and suffering threaten humankind. But the combination of his immersion in the Scriptures and the decision to return to Germany the second time without any illusions as to the probable consequences resulted in a penetrating grasp of Jesus' words:

> And I say to you, My friends, don't fear those who kill the body, and after that can do nothing more. But I will show you the One to fear; fear Him who has the authority to throw people into hell after death. Yes, I say to you, this is the One to fear! Aren't five sparrows sold for two pennies? Yet not one of them is forgotten in God's sight. Indeed, the hairs of your head are all counted. Don't be afraid; you are worth more than many sparrows. (Luke 12:4–7)

The ultimate impotence of suffering and death has been exposed. Jesus Christ, by his death and resurrection, has made a public show of this ultimate impotence. Furthermore, in Jesus Christ, God has taken upon himself the suffering of the world and used it as the means for the world's redemption. We now live in the midst of suffering but with the demonstration of its limit behind us and with the promise of its end before us. We have seen its redemptive potential in the crucifixion of our Lord. In addition (and this is crucial for understanding Bonhoeffer's conception of the Christian life) those who are called to follow Christ may expect to suffer as he did. His witnesses can expect a rude reception in the world. But even in the midst of this suffering—indeed, only from the perspective gained in the midst of witness-induced suffering—disciples learn of the freedom and joy only Christ gives to his followers:

> There remains an experience of incomparable value,
> namely that we have learned to see the great events of world

history from below, from the perspective of those who are excluded, under suspicion, ill-treated, powerless, oppressed and scorned, in short, those who suffer. . . . Our perception of what is great, human, just and merciful has become clearer, freer, more incorruptible, indeed, personal suffering is a more useful key, a more fruitful principle for opening up the world in thought and action than personal happiness.[122]

A Short Theological Postscript

Where I Stand on Bonhoeffer the Theologian

I agree with Eberhard Bethge that Bonhoeffer's work is characterized more by continuity than by either obvious development or discontinuity. Accordingly I shall not feel obliged to find corroboration of earlier statements in later works when stating Bonhoeffer's position. I do recognize shifts in emphasis and interest in Bonhoeffer's thinking but not radical breaks with his earlier views, especially from around 1931 on. We should remember that Bonhoeffer was only thirty-nine years of age at the time of his execution. I agree with the consensus of many that Bonhoeffer's thought was not fully developed. He was a young thinker, not a mature theologian; and he often wrote while burdened with pastoral duties and deep involvement in political and social matters and of course, ultimately, the conspiracy to assassinate Adolf Hitler. These factors account better for disconnects and even occasional contradictions present in his work than any division of his work into supposedly early and late periods. In my estimation the burden rests squarely with those who would argue for major shifts in Bonhoeffer's thinking.

I also agree with Bethge that Karl Barth was the one great theological discovery and theological influence of Bonhoeffer's life. It may be obvious to those conversant with Barth that much that I find attractive in Bonhoeffer's thinking for evangelicals often has its source in Barth's influence.

Is Bonhoeffer a Liberal?

Bonhoeffer's story has, understandably, piqued the interest of Christians and non-Christians alike, including evangelicals. However, Bonhoeffer was a pastor and theologian before he joined the conspiracy to assassinate Hitler, and use of his writings has been decidedly more attractive to theological liberals and progressives than to evangelicals. The typical explanation for this state of affairs tends to run something like this: Bonhoeffer was influenced by liberals such as his neighbor, the great Adolph von Harnack, and especially by Swiss theologian Karl Barth, the so-called father of neoorthodoxy, which is, well, liberalism lite or perhaps, liberalism in disguise—the liberal wolf decked out in evangelical sheep's clothing.

My view is that there is some truth in all of this but not very much. Evangelical critiques of both Barth and Bonhoeffer have often been a little too quick and dirty by my estimation. Still, it will not be my purpose to make either Karl Barth or Dietrich Bonhoeffer walk and talk like American evangelicals. They were not. From the perspective of the evangelical, both men display certain glaring weaknesses and blind spots. So why bid evangelicals come sit at the feet of Bonhoeffer? Because what Bonhoeffer got right belongs to all Christians and has, I believe, particular relevance for evangelicals. We evangelicals have our own blind spots to dispel, and sometimes the critique most needed cannot come from within our own ranks.

Was Bonhoeffer a liberal? My short answer to this question is no. Bonhoeffer studied under the star proponents of Protestant liberalism at the University of Berlin—Harnack, Holl, and Seeberg. But during the 1924–25 winter semester, he encountered the theology of Karl Barth, which involved an onslaught upon original, Schleiermacherian liberalism. For Bonhoeffer, liberalism never recovered. Ten months before his execution, writing from his prison cell, Bonhoeffer continued his exploration of the failures of liberalism: "The weakness of liberal theology was that it conceded to the world the right to determine Christ's place in the world." Barth's fingerprints are obvious. My short answer to the related question of whether Bonhoeffer is neoorthodox is that the term neoorthodoxy lacks clarity and proves largely unhelpful to those wishing to understand Bonhoeffer's views and significance. Within his own contexts he certainly belongs to a back-to-the-Bible movement of sorts initiated by Karl Barth and he understood better than some contemporary evangelicals the essential nature of the Protestant liberalism he opposed. Without question, in his life we are confronted with a follower of Jesus prepared to die rather than abandon his Lord. Dietrich Bonhoeffer has much to teach us, and we evangelicals need not put our heads in the sand to sit at his feet for a spell.

ENDNOTES

1. Dietrich Bonhoeffer, *The Cost of Discipleship*, trans. by R. H. Fuller (New York: Macmillan, 1949), 99.

2. Eberhard Bethge, *Dietrich Bonhoeffer: Man of Vision, Man of Courage* (New York: Harper & Row, 1977), 45. This treatment by Bethge, Bonhoeffer's close friend and fellow conspirator, who also married Bonhoeffer's niece Renate, is the most comprehensive biography available and the standard in the field.

3. Bethge, *Dietrich Bonhoeffer*, 22.

4. Bethge, *Dietrich Bonhoeffer*, 42.

5. Bethge, *Dietrich Bonhoeffer*, 76.

6. Bethge, *Dietrich Bonhoeffer*, 93.

7. Bethge, *Dietrich Bonhoeffer*, 132.

8. Bethge, *Dietrich Bonhoeffer*, 153–56. See also Bonhoeffer's letter to his brother-in-law and good friend Rüdiger Schleicher in *Dietrich Bonhoeffer: Meditating on the Word*, trans. and ed. by David McI. Gracie, 42–48.

9. Eberhard Bethge, *Costly Grace: An Illustrated Introduction to Dietrich Bonhoeffer* (New York: Harper & Row, 1979), 56.

10. Bethge, *Costly Grace*, 208.

11. Clifford Green, ed., *Karl Barth: Theologian of Freedom* (London: Collins, 1989), 149.

12. Green, *Karl Barth*, 150.

13. Bethge, *Costly Grace*, 67.

14. Eberhard Busch, *Karl Barth: His Life from Letters and Autobiographical Texts*, trans. by John Bowden (Philadelphia: Fortress, 1976), 233.

15. Bethge, *Dietrich Bonhoeffer*, 556.

16. Bethge, *Dietrich Bonhoeffer*, 585

17. Bethge, *Dietrich Bonhoeffer*, 632.

18. Bethge, *Dietrich Bonhoeffer*, 633.

19. Rebecca Brooks Gruver, *An American History* 2nd ed. (Reading, Mass.: Addison-Wesley, 1976), 875.

20. Bethge, *Dietrich Bonhoeffer*, 638.

21. Bethge, *Dietrich Bonhoeffer*, 673.

22. William L. Shirer, *The Rise and Fall of the Third Reich: A History of Nazi Germany* (New York: Simon and Schuster, 1960), 1019.

23. Shirer, *Rise and Fall*, 1021.

24. Bethge, *Dietrich Bonhoeffer*, 736.

25. Bethge, *Dietrich Bonhoeffer*, 720–21.

26. Bethge, *Dietrich Bonhoeffer*, 701.

27. Dietrich Bonhoeffer, *Letters and Papers from Prison: the Enlarged Edition*, ed. by Eberhard Bethge (New York: Macmillan, 1953), 174.

28. Shirer, *Rise and Fall*, 1041.

29. Bethge, *Dietrich Bonhoeffer*, 830–31.

30. This is the title of chapter 2 in Karl Barth's *The Word of God and the Word of Man*, trans. by Douglas Horton (New York: Harper and Brothers, 1957).

31. Bethge, *Dietrich Bonhoeffer*, 153.

32. Bethge, *Dietrich Bonhoeffer*, 154.

33. Bethge, *Dietrich Bonhoeffer*, 154.

34. Dietrich Bonhoeffer, *Meditating on the Word*, trans. and ed. by David McL. Gracie (Cambridge, Mass.: Cowley, 1986), 43.

35. Bethge, *Dietrich Bonhoeffer*, 153–56.

36. Bethge, *Dietrich Bonhoeffer*, 155.

37. Bonhoeffer, *Meditating*, 46.

38. Bethge, *Dietrich Bonhoeffer*, 43.

39. Bonhoeffer, *Discipleship*, 99.

40. Dietrich Bonhoeffer, *Ethics*, trans. by Neville Horton Smith (New York: Touchstone, 1957), 192.

41. Quoted by James Burtness in *Shaping the Future: The Ethics of Dietrich Bonhoeffer* (Philadelphia: Fortress, 1985), 14.

42. Bonhoeffer, *Ethics*, 186.

43. Bonhoeffer, *Ethics*, 192.

44. Quoted in Gerhard Jacobi, *I Knew Dietrich Bonhoeffer*, ed. by Wolf Dieter Zimmerman and Ronald Gregor Smith (London: Collins, 1966), 46.

45. Bonhoeffer, *Ethics*, 19.

46. J. I. Packer, *Keep in Step with the Spirit* (Grand Rapids: Revell, 1984), 46.

47. Bethge, *Dietrich Bonhoeffer*, 49.

48. Bonhoeffer, *Discipleship*.

49. Bonhoeffer, *Discipleship*, 252.

50. Bonhoeffer, *Discipleship*, 252.

51. Raymond E. Brown, *The Gospel According to John*, Vol. 29A of *The Anchor Bible* (Garden City, N.Y.: Doubleday, 1970), 714.

52. Brown, *John*, 715.

53. Dietrich Bonhoeffer, *Life Together*, trans. by John W. Doberstein (San Francisco: Harper & Row, 1954), 81–82.

54. Find numerous occurrences in Bonhoeffer's *The Communion of Saints: a Dogmatic Inquiry into the Sociology of the Church* (New York; Harper & Row, 1960) and *Act and Being*, trans. by Bernard Noble (New York: Harper & Row, 1961).

55. Bethge, *Dietrich Bonhoeffer*, 58.

56. Bonhoeffer, *Discipleship*, 105.

57. Bonhoeffer, *Discipleship*, 106–107.

58. Bonhoeffer, *Discipleship*, 106.

59. Dietrich Bonhoeffer, *Creation and Fall* and *Temptation: Two Biblical Studies*, trans. by John C. Fletcher (New York: Macmillan, 1937), 37–38.

60. Bonhoeffer, *Life Together*, 19–20.

61. David S. Dockery, "A Theology for the Church," *Midwestern Journal of Theology*, vol. 1, no, 1 & 2, (Spring, 2003), 18.

62. Bonhoeffer, *Life Together*, 26.

63. Bonhoeffer, *Discipleship*, 47.

64. Bonhoeffer, *Life Together*, 31.

65. *Luther's Works*, Harold J. Grimm, ed., vol. 31, *Career of the Reformer: 1* (Philadelphia: Fortress, 1957), 25.

66. Bethge, *Dietrich Bonhoeffer,* 39.

67. Bonhoeffer, *Life Together,* 105.

68. Dietrich Bonhoeffer, *True Patriotism: Letters, Lectures and Notes 1939–1945,* ed. by Edwin H. Robertson and trans. by Edwin H. Robertson and John Bowden (New York: Harper & Row, 1973), 187.

69. Bonhoeffer, *Letters and Papers,* 369.

70. Bethge, *Dietrich Bonhoeffer,* 154–55.

71. Bonhoeffer, *Life Together,* 26.

72. See David F. Wells's two volumes: *No Place for Truth: or, Whatever Happened to Evangelical Theology?* (Grand Rapids: Eerdmans, 1993) and *God in the Wasteland: The Reality of Truth in a World of Fading Dreams* (Grand Rapids: Eerdmans, 1994).

73. Dietrich Bonhoeffer, *No Rusty Swords: Letters, Lectures and Notes 1928–1936,* ed. by Edwin H. Robertson, trans. by Edwin H. Robertson and John Bowden (London: Collins, 1965), 309–10.

74. Bonhoeffer, *Discipleship,* 51.

75. Green, *Karl Barth,* 149.

76. Bonhoeffer, *No Rusty Swords,* 308. Emphasis added.

77. Bonhoeffer, *Discipleship,* 284.

78. Bonhoeffer, *Discipleship,* 283–84.

79. Bethge, *Discipleship,* 93.

80. Dietrich Bonhoeffer, *Who Is Christ for Us?,* ed. and trans. by Craig Nessan and Renate Wind (Minneapolis: Fortress, 2002), 38–39.

81. Dietrich Bonhoeffer, *Creation and Fall,* 69–87.

82. Dietrich Bonhoeffer, *Letters and Papers,* 326–27.

83. Rick Warren, *The Purpose Driven Life: What on Earth Am I Here For?* (Grand Rapids: Zondevan, 2002), 17.

84. Bethge, *Dietrich Bonhoeffer,* 65.

85. Dietrich Bonhoeffer, *Ethics,* 236.

86. Bethge, *Dietrich Bonhoeffer,* 232.

87. Busch, *Karl Barth,* 245.

88. Bethge, *Dietrich Bonhoeffer,* 297–98.

89. Green, *Karl Barth,* 149.

90. See in *Natural Theology: Comprising "Nature and Grace" by Dr. Emil Brunner and the Reply "No!" by Dr. Karl Barth,* trans. by Peter Fraenkel (Eugene, Oreg.: Wipf & Stock, 2002).

91. Green, *Karl Barth,* 149.

92. Green, *Karl Barth,* 149.

93. Green, *Karl Barth*, 150.

94. Jean Bethke Elshtain, *Just War Against Terror: The Burden of American Power in a Violent World* (New York: Basic Books, 2003), 24, 25.

95. Bonhoeffer, *Ethics*, 174.

96. Bonhoeffer, *Ethics*, 174.

97. Bonhoeffer, *Ethics*, 174.

98. Bonhoeffer, *Ethics*, 174.

99. Bonhoeffer, *Life Together*, 84.

100. Dockery, "A Theology for the Church," *Midwestern Journal of Theology*, vol. 1, no., 1 & 2 (Spring, 2003), 18.

101. Tertullian, *The Ante-Nicene Fathers*, Vol. III, ed. by rev. Alexander Roberts and James Donaldson (Grand Rapids: Eerdmans, 1986), 55.

102. Bonhoeffer, *Letters and Papers*, 370–72.

103. Bonhoeffer, *Life Together*, 13.

104. Bonhoeffer, *Life Together*, 84.

105. Bonhoeffer, *Ethics*, 50.

106. Bonhoeffer, *Ethics*, 40–51.

107. Dietrich Bonhoeffer, *Psalms: the Prayerbook of the Bible*, trans. by James H. Burtness (Minneapolis: Augsburg. Publishing House, 1970), 31–32. See also Bonhoeffer, *Ethics*, 272–81.

108. Bonhoeffer, *Discipleship*, 242.

109. Bonhoeffer, *Discipleship*, 242.

110. Bonhoeffer, *Discipleship*, 242–43.

111. Bethge, *Dietrich Bonhoeffer*, 61.

112. Bonhoeffer, *Letters and Papers*, 15–16.

113. Bonhoeffer, *Discipleship*, 233, 238.

114. Bonhoeffer, *Letters and Papers*, 336–37.

115. Søren Kierkegaard, *Fear and Trembling and the Sickness Unto Death*, trans. by Walter Lowrie (Princeton, N.J.: Princeton University Press, 1954), 21–139.

116. Bonhoeffer, *Patriotism*, 189.

117. Quoted in *Dietrich Bonhoeffer*, The Modern Spirituality Series, ed. by Aileen Taylor (Springfield, Ill.: Templegate, 1992), 68.

118. Taylor, *Dietrich Bonhoeffer*, 70.

119. Bonhoeffer, *Discipleship*, 45–60.

120. Bonhoeffer, *Patriotism*, 189.

121. Bonhoeffer, *Patriotism*, 189.

122. Taylor, *Dietrich Bonhoeffer*, 78.